SAN ANTONIO
AND ITS BEGINNINGS

comprising

**THE FOUR NUMBERS OF
THE SAN ANTONIO SERIES
WITH APPENDIX**

by

FREDERICK C. CHABOT

SAN ANTONIO:

ARTES GRAFICAS PRINTING CO.

1936

Published, April, 1936

ST. FRANCIS OF ASSISI

CONTENTS

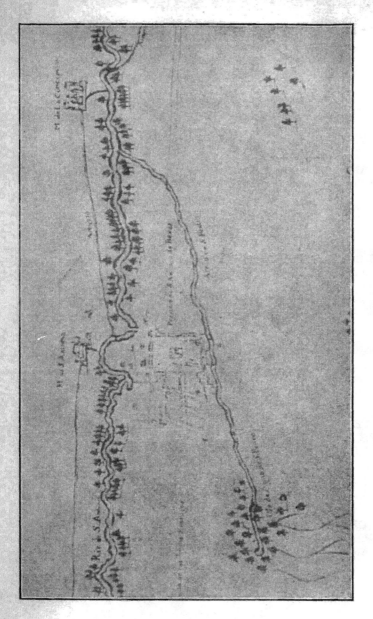

MAP OF THE PRESIDIO OF SAN ANTONIO DE BEXAR AND ITS MISSIONS

By Capt. Luis Antonio Menchaca, 1764. Original in John Carter Brown Library.

SAN ANTONIO
Of the 17th, 18th and 19th Centuries

B ACK in the century of the Conquest, the Spaniards were not long in exploring the vast territory lying between the Rio Grande and the eastern boundaries of our present state of Texas. The Aztec Empire, at the beginning of the 16th century had its highways far beyond the boundaries of the empire, and it is not unlikely that the victorious armies returned to the capital of Mexico with treasures and prisoners, and with tales of adventure. This was all one small part of the great struggle between Spain, France and England for possession of America.

The famous *Relación* of Cabeza de Vaca, published in 1542, after six years captivity among the Texas Indians, is one of the earliest documents giving us details of those bygone days and tribes. Later in the century, the Venerable Mother María de Agreda wrote from her convent regarding the kingdom of the *Ticlas* or *Theas*, which she stated was eastward from the *Gran Quivira*. From these tribes the province took its name: *Theas* being the Spanish spelling of the Indian word, which probably meant friends, and through the customary interchange of letters, became *Téjas* and then *Texas*.

The first formal expedition was under Alonzo de León, and took place in 1689. A second, under the same leader, in 1690, established the mission and village of *San Francisco de los Tejas*, in the presence of the Chief of all the Texas nations. A third, under Domingo de Terán, in 1691, reached the Cadodachos River, and established a Royal *Almacén* (Warehouse) at San Pedro de Texas, where many Indians were baptized. During this expedition Joseph de Urrutia visited the site of present San Antonio, which was then an Indian village.

These 17th century expeditions were not long lasting, for toward the end of 1692, a contagious disease spread among the natives, the seasons were severe, with the loss of crops and cattle, and the Spanish soldiers outraged the Indian women, which caused open rebellion. Then came news of French attacks. So the missions were abandoned and the padres returned to Mexico. Urrutia however, with three companions, preferred to remain among his friends the Indians. Then followed a relatively inactive period of preparation, which resulted in permanent Spanish settlements in Texas. The following chronological arrangements of events should facilitate the reader in grasping a general conception of the beginning and growth of San Antonio, whose history is so rich in color and romance.

1714   St. Denis, a Frenchman from Louisiana, establishing trade relations with Mexico, approved the site as suitable to a city.

1715   Spanish families were already permanently settled here.

1716   The Domingo Ramón Expedition, accompanied by St. Denis, established a *presidio* or military post here. At the same time, the Queretaran Father Olivares began his missionary activities here, in a *jacal* or thatched hut, with three or four converted Indians, calling the establishment the mission of *San Antonio de Padua*.

1718   The Alarcón Expedition reenforced the presidio, and ten soldiers with their families were recognized as the beginning of a *villa*, or settlement. The San Antonio de Padua mission was officially founded under the name of San Antonio de Valero, in honor of the viceroy of the time, the Marquis of Valero, when the San Francisco Solano mission was transferred from the Rio Grande and merged with it.

1720   San José mission was founded by Father Margil de Jesús.

1722   The Marquis of Aguayo, governor of the province, and leader of an expedition (1719-1722) after driving the French from Texas, and reestablishing the missions in east Texas, removed the primitive presidio to the better protected location, the site of the present Military Plaza, at the entrance to the loop in the river, where fortifications and permanent stone buildings were constructed, and where the irrigation system was improved.

1726   The population of San Antonio totaled 200, including forty-five military and four civilian settlers, with their families.

1727   The garrisons of Texas were reduced in spite of the new peril, the Apaches. New plans for colonization with families were under consideration.

1731   The three Queretaran missions of east Texas, (Conception, San Juan and the Espada) were removed to the San Antonio. Sixteen families, with eleven distinct family names, including 52 persons, arrived from the Canary Islands, by way of Mexico, and founded the villa of San Fernando, around the site of the present Main Plaza, which was the capital of the province.

1734   During the Sandoval regime, the Governor's residence was established in San Antonio, and many troops came with him from the Spanish settlement of the Adaes of east Texas and were stationed here. The *Comandancia* of the presidio, where the governor resided, became known as the Governor's Palace. The corner stone of the San Fernando parish church (the present cathedral) was laid during this year.

1743   The first intelligence of the Comanches was now received. The total Indian population of the five missions on the San Antonio was about 814.

1758   A political and military *junta* was held in San Antonio, subsequent to the discovery of the Almagre mines, for the purpose of organizing a campaign against the Indian Nations of the North.

1759   The Bishop of Guadalajara visited San Antonio and confirmed many of the inhabitants.

1760 . The first text book for Mission Espada, in the Spanish and Indian dialect, was published in Mexico.

1761   Laws of reform were passed, prohibiting loitering, carrying arms, drinking and gambling, *fandangos,* the public grazing of animals, and the manufacture of aguardiente. Fences were ordered put up, and the farmers were warned against disposing of their means to the extent of leaving families in want.

1762   San Antonio had 103 inhabitants ready for military service. The *Cuerpo de Guardia* or military guard was now composed of 20 regular salaried men.

1768   English traders had penetrated as far as the Texas border.

1770   Demecier reported danger from the English. The population of San Fernando, the capital of the province, and only formal settlement in it, numbered 870 souls, as many had been killed and others expelled by the incessant hostilities of the savages.

1774   Military forces were concentrated at Bexar under the Command of Governor Ripperdá. They numbered 500.

1778 · · A bando (edict) proclaimed all unbranded cattle property of the king.

1779   A monthly mail service was established for Texas.

1789   A school was founded in San Antonio by De La Mata.

1790   The "Republicans" of San Antonio had the audacity of holding a junta without permission from the authorities. The hangers-on of the deserted presidio of the Adaes arrived in San Antonio and settled here.

1793   It was necessary to obtain a special permit to go fishing, to gather nuts, to hunt bears and to kill unbranded cattle.

1794   Philip Nolan visited in San Antonio. There were 3,417 inhabitants in the capital and three towns of the province.

1803   The Company of the Alamo of Parras was stationed here, at the old San Antonio de Valero Mission or "Alamo".

1813   San Antonio surrendered to the Americans under Kemper, as a result of the defeat of the Spaniards on the Rocillo. The Royalists under Elisondo were defeated, and the Americans returned to San Antonio. Toledo was elected commander-in-chief. The Americans or Army of the North were defeated on the Medina, and only 93 Americans were able to escape to Natchitoches. Arredondo marched triumphantly into San Antonio and sought revenge on the Republicans.

1814   San Antonio had become a desolate place, suffering from the heel of a ruthless tyrant within, and surrounded by ferocious Indians without. Prices became prohibitive and food very scarce.

1816   By this time San Antonio was almost abandoned.

1819   A serious flood took place on July 5th, and many removed to the settlement around the Alamo, on the east side of the river, which was called *La Villita* (the little town).

1820   Moses Austin petitioned the Governor in San Antonio for a permit to settle families in Texas. The whole population of the province, not including the Indians, was not more than 4,000.

1823   Subsequent to the defeat of the Royalists in Mexico, and the end of their campaigns, the old inhabitants of San Antonio returned, and with a large number of troops and new immigrants, the town recovered its importance. The population of San Antonio had now increased to about 5,000.

1824   Texas and Coahuila were united, and San Antonio lost her importance as a state capital. She was reduced to the capital of a department.

1825   This is called the year of American immigration into Texas.

1828   The first American school was established in San Antonio, in consequence of the increase of her English speaking population.

1829   McGloin and McMullen were among the first to inaugurate a four years Irish immigration.

1830 -   Though a federal decree forbade immigration from the states, Americans continued to come into Texas, and Texas lands were recklessly granted by Mexican authorities to their favorites. Veramendi, whose daughter Ursula married James Bowie, was elected vice-governor, which was favorable toward the American colonists. A custom house was now established in the district of Bexar. Owing to the increase of colonists, the department of Texas was divided into two districts, San Antonio remaining the capital of

Bexar, and Nacogdoches becoming the seat of the political chief of the eastern district.

1831　James and Resin Bowie, the latter the inventor of the "Bowie Knife", were now active in San Antonio and vicinity.

1834　The first strictly revolutionary meeting to discuss Texas independence from Mexico was held in San Antonio.

1835　An attempt to disarm the Americans at Gonzales was the inauguration of actual warfare. General Cos was driven from San Antonio by the "Western Army" (Americans) under Old Ben Milam. The capitulations were signed in what is known as the "Cos House" on Villita Street. Samuel A. Maverick arrived in San Antonio. Johnson assumed command of the Alamo, with a sufficient force to defend it. Bexar, no longer the Mexican stronghold, now became the "key to the situation in Texas."

1836　The Mexican forces concentrated on San Antonio, and Travis and the few Americans in the place retreated to the Alamo which was stormed by the entire Mexican forces, under Santa Anna; and then followed the Battle of San Jacinto and Texas Independence. During the Republic, San Antonio was the capital of Bexar County. Her first mayor of the period was John W. Smith.

1838　The General Land Office opened in San Antonio which attracted a very undesirable element to the place.

1839　Samuel A. Maverick was mayor of San Antonio.

1840　"The Court House Fight" or "Break of '40" which was an attempt of the Americans to hold the Indians in hostage for American prisoners in their possession, resulted in deliberate and organized Indian depredations. This old Court House was the *Casa Real,* which was located on the northeast corner of Main Plaza, and Market Street of today.

1842　General Vasquez dashed into San Antonio and departed with the "treasures" and Mexican sympathizers. Upon the approach of General Woll and the regular Mexican army, the Americans fortified the Maverick home, which overlooked Main Plaza, (northeast corner of present Commerce St. and the Plaza) and attempted to defend the town. They were all imprisoned and taken to Mexico where they were placed in the famous Perote Castle.

Texas was annexed to the Union in 1845, but the government of the Republic continued until 1846. American troops were temporarily quartered in Military Plaza, until Major Babitt occupied the Alamo as a Quartermaster's depot, where this branch of the service continued until 1878, excepting the Civil War period. In

1849 General Worth resided in the old John James home on the northwest corner of Commerce and Presa Streets, while the troops were in temporary barracks in the Conception Mission, and at the head of the river, at the springs which became known as Worth Springs.

In the 50's John and William Vance had officers quarters and barracks built at the site of the present corner of Houston and St. Mary's Streets, which was conveniently located for water supply from the river. These buildings were first occupied in 1856. They were also occupied as Confederate Headquarters. The French Building during the Civil War, was known as the "Confederate Aid Store." In 1865 it was Federal Headquarters. In 1868 it was used as an annex to the Court House.

The old Maverick Hotel on Houston St., was originally constructed for Federal Headquarters and occupied by General Ord in June of 1875. During the same month the Quartermaster's Depot on the Hill was completed. The headquarters building of Fort Sam Houston was commenced at the orders of Major Belknap on May 6, 1875.

The United States arsenal was removed from a building near the Veramendi House on Soledad Street after the war, to the present site on South Flores St. where building had commenced November 1, 1859.

The first newspaper published in English in San Antonio, was *The West Texas* or *The Western Texan*. It was printed in the old Mill northeast of the Mill Bridge on Navarro St. This first weekly made its appearance in 1848. It was succeeded by the *Ledger* in 1859, established by Jacob Walker and subsequently owned by Van Derlip and Hewitt, who sold it to Michael Burks, who converted it into a daily in 1856. Shortly after it was owned by William Maverick and located in the old Veramendi house.

The *Purísima Concepción*, known as "the first mission" was originally founded for the Asinais Indians by the Domingo Ramón Expedition in 1716 in east Texas, beyond the Angelina River, and under the protection of an adjacent presidio or military post. It was removed to the San Antonio in 1731.

The *San José*, commonly called "the second mission" because of its relative location in the vicinity of San Antonio, was founded by Father Margil de Jesús in 1720, while he was a refugee in San Antonio, awaiting the Aguayo Expedition, which was to drive out the French and reestablish the missions in east Texas. It was named *San José de San Miguel de Aguayo* in honor of the governor, the Marquis of Aguayo. There is a local tradition that the beautiful south window of the baptistry was carved by Pedro Huizar, whose ancestor is said to have worked on the Alcazar of Seville. Wealth, beauty and art strove to make this kingly mission the wonder of its day.

The San Juan Capistrano, commonly known as "the third mission" was founded in 1716 for the Nazones Indians, when it was called *San José de los Nazones*. But when it was removed to the San Antonio in 1731, where there was already a mission by the name of San José, it was called San Juan Capistrano, in honor of the Franciscan, Santo Giovanni, native of Capistrano, in the Abruzzi in Italy. The frescoes on this mission gave satisfaction to the Indians' love of color. Nearby are the ruins of an old aqueduct, a series of low, massive arches.

The *San Francisco de la Espada*, known as "the fourth mission" was originally the San Francisco de los Neches, , and dates back to the very beginning of Texas history. In San Antonio it was named in honor of Saint Francis of Assissi, the founder of the great order of Franciscans; and according to tradition, the old tower being built in the form of the hilt of a sword, it was called *de la Espada* (of the sword). It is also said that the mortar was mixed with asses' milk . This mission has the distinction of having used the first text book in the province of Texas; written by Father Bartholome Garcia of the mission, in Spanish and in the most common Indian dialect of the vicinity, and published in Mexico in 1760.

The rapid growth of San Antonio dates from 1876, when the first railway (Sunset Route) entered the city. From 1879-1880 to 1887, the population increased from 14,894 to 42,570; from 1900 to 1910, the population increased from 53,321 to 96,614. Today the population of San Antonio exceeds two hundred thousand.

The Governors' Palace – San Antonio

The Presidio of Texas

A RMORIAL BEARINGS, in all ages and in all quarters of the world have been adopted, so history generally informs us, as distinguishing symbols, by tribes or nations, by families or by chieftains. Greek and Roman poets describe the devices borne on the shields of heroes. The charges of the shield were also found displayed on the knight's long surcoat, his "coat of arms," on his banner or pennon; on the trappers of his horse and even upon the peaks of his saddle. "The eagle of the emperors may well be as ancient a bearing as any in Europe, seeing that Charlemagne is said, as the successor of the Caesars, to have used the eagle as his badge. The emperor Henry III (1039-1056) has the sceptre on his seal surmounted by an eagle . . . . The double-headed eagle is not seen on an imperial seal until after 1414, when the bird with one neck becomes the recognized arms of the king of the Romans."

The ancient Aztec chiefs of Mexico, before the Spanish Conquest, carried shields and banners, some of whose devices showed after the fashion of a phonetic writing, the names of their bearers; and "the eagle on the new banner of Mexico may be traced to the eagle that was once carved over the palace of Moctezuma." It is recorded too, that the Indians of Chile carved and painted double-headed eagles, long before the advent of the Spaniards in their lands.

A Habsburg and Emperor, as King of Spain, accounts for the double-headed eagle as a support to Spanish arms. Charles of Habsburg, born at Ghent in 1500, was the son of Philip of Burgundy and Joanna, third child of Ferdinand and Isabella. At the death of his grandfather Ferdinand, in 1516, he became king of Spain as Charles I. At the death of Maximilian, he succeeded to the inheritance of the Habsburgs. His grandfather "had also intended that he should succeed as emperor. In spite of the rivalry of Francis I, of France, and the opposition of Pope Leo X, "pecuniary corruption and national feeling combined to secure his election in 1519." Charles was crowned at Aix on the 23rd of October, 1520. His arms were those of his paternal line, quartered with those of Spain. The supports were the imperial eagle.

Charles abdicated and was succeeded by his son Philip. The period of one hundred and two years (1598-1700), covered by the reigns of Philip III, Philip IV and Charles II, "was one of decadence, ending in intellectual, moral and material degradation. The dynasty continued to make the maintenance of the rights and interests of the House of Austria its main objects . . . " Upon the death of Charles II, without issue, on November 1, 1700, the duke of Anjou was proclaimed King, as Philip V, in accordance with the decision of his grandfather, Louis XIV, of France. This was the beginning of the Bourbon Dynasty in Spain; and the War of the Spanish Succession, which terminated only 13 years later, by the peace of Utrecht. The arms of Philip V were the ancient arms of the kings of France, the blue shield with three golden fleurs-de-lys (the flower, whose name, as "Fleur-de-Loys," had played upon the epithet name, *Florus*, of Louis le Jeune), surmounting the quarterings of Castile and Leon. Among his numerous titles, Philip V styled himself Archduke of Austria and Count of Habsburg. It would seem that either through political malice, or to surprise the scientific world, the viceroy, the Marquis of Valero, reported that a race of double-headed eagles was native of Mexico. He sent one such specimen, embalmed, from Mexico, to the Convent of the Escurial in Spain.

"The reign of Charles was in America the age of conquest and organization. Upon his accession the settlements upon the mainland were insignificant; by 1556 conquest was practically complete, and civil and ecclesiastical government firmly established. Actual expansion was the work of great adventurers starting on their own impulse from the older colonies . . . "

The map showing the Coasts from *Nombre de Dios* to Florida, dated 1519, reproduced in the *Early Texas Album*, notes the discovery of Florida, then called *Bimyny*, by Juan Ponce de León; and the discoveries of Francisco de Garay, which followed to the west, including *La Bahia del Espiritu Santo*. Garay, the first governor of Amichel, was appointed governor of Santiago (1521), the Indian *Jaymaca*, "the island of springs," discovered by Columbus in 1494, and called by him, *Santiago*. The jurisdiction of the government of Santiago extended over the territory of present Texas. Garay was captured by Cortés, near Tampico, and died in prison in Mexico City. The territory from Tampico to the River of Palms was granted to Cortés, with the meaning name of *Victoria Garayana*. The balance of the territory, from the River of Palms (Rio Grande) to Juan Ponce (Florida), was named *Río de las Palmas*, and was granted to Pánfilo de Narvaez, who in 1527, sailed with five ships and a force of 600 men to take possession of what he thought was fabulous wealth. Continuing the voyage from Florida for Mexico, Narvaez perished with his boat at sea. This was when his lieutenant, Cabeza de Vaca, with his companions, reached land and made his way across Texas to the Gulf of California. The next governor of that region including Río de las Palmas, Florida, the territory explored by Ayon, and Cuba, was Fernando de Soto, who excited by the reports of De Vaca and others as to the wealth of Florida, armed four ships, and sailed from San Lucar in April of 1538 going first to Havana, then landing (1539) in Espíritu Santo Bay, on the west coast of the present state of Florida. After nearly four years of fruitless search of gold, De Soto died (1542) and his body was sunk in the waters of the Mississippi.

In the 2nd decade of the 17th century Venerable Mother María de Agreda wrote from her convent regarding the kingdom of the *Ticlas* or *Théas,* which she stated was eastward from the *Gran Quivira.* From these Indians the province of Texas ultimately took its name, *Theas* being the Spanish spelling of the Indian word which probably meant friends, or confederation, and through the customary interchange of letters, became *Téjas* and then *Texas.*

Those stragglers who remained of the proud Coronado Expedition, returned to Mexico in 1542, with every appearance of dismal failure. They told tales of adventure and mineral wealth, however, which inspired the descendants of the Conquerors to continue ever onward. The Bosque *entrada of* 1674 was one of the activities foreshadowing the gradual extension of missionary activities for the settlement of Coahuila and Nuevo León across the Rio Grande into Texas.

The movements of the French, and rumors of their activities in Texas, excited Spanish officials. In consequence, Captain Alonzo de León was dispatched on his first expedition, in 1685. A second expedition was no more successful than the first. Persistent rumors of French activities provoked a third expedition, which set out in March of 1689. This time the Spaniards arrived at the Bay of St. Louis, and discovered the desolate remains of La Salle's unfortunate colony. De León, with some of his men explored the interior, and followed the course of the San Antonio River. In 1690 a more formal expedition returned to St. Louis, and completely destroyed the ruins of the old fort. They continued on to eastern frontiers, and founded the first Texas mission, *San Francisco de los Téjas.*

The viceroy, the Count of Galve, impressed with the natural resources of the province of the Téjas, and with the desire of the Indians to have missionaries sent them, appointed Domingo de Terán de los Ríos, governor and commander of the region. Royal Cédulas were issued in 1690 for the pacification and reduction of the province. Terán and his expedition left Coahuila in May of 1691, with instructions to thoroughly explore the province and to drive from it, any foreign intruders. They visited the Indian village at the present site of San Antonio, and arrived as far east as mission San Francisco, where they established a Royal Warehouse at *San Pedro de Théxas,* in the vicinity of the San Andrés or Cadodachos River. The loss of this *Almacén* by fire, along with the illness of the Commander, Salinas, caused the abandonment of the project. When the expedition returned to Mexico, the Alferez called "Aerratto" was left with nine soldiers, to protect the eight ministers of the church. This then, was the first attempt of the Spaniards, to establish a permanent military post in the territory of the Texas.

The subsequent and total abandonment of the missions in 1693, left the province, it would seem, to the "undisturbed possession of the Indians." At this time the brave Captain Urrutia came to the foreground in Texas history. He refused to desert his friends the Indians, but remained among them, and incidentally prepared himself for greater services to the Spanish Crown.

It was not until 1707 that another military expedition entered Texas territory. Diego Ramón, with his company of men, was instructed, not to drive out the French, but to pursue and chastise the *Rancheria Grande* Indians, who had caused disturbances at the missions.

In February of 1716, Captain Domingo Ramón, son of the former, began his formidable journey to the Province of Texas. On the 14th of May the expedition reached "a spring, level with the ground, which they called *San Pedro*. It was large enough to supply a city. They entered a beautiful spot on the San Antonio River, where there were walnuts, vines, willows, elms, and other kinds of trees. They crossed the river which was of good size, the water being up to the stirrups but no deeper. They went up to the hunt a good place and found a fine one where there was a beautiful little open place with wood and pasturage. They explored the head of the river and found hemp three varas high and flax four spans high, according to the estimate of twelve experienced overseas men. Fish enough for everybody was caught and it was seen that water could be easily taken from the river for irrigation. The 15th, was spent in this place because it was suited to rest the horses, and in order to celebrate the day of San Ysidro, as was done." The expedition continued to east Texas and on the last day of June, set up camp a short distance from the San Francisco mission.

Ramón postponed the establishment of presidio until he could find a suitable location for it, and in order that he might immediately proceed with the locating of the missions. According to a report of 1740, the Presidio called San Antonio was located in 1716, in compliance with orders from His Majesty, on the banks of the river with the same name; and to the east of said river, and presidio, somewhat more to the north, a mission had been established with the same name.

The Ramón Expedition found the rivals of Spain facing aggressively westward, and now the Spanish government realized that to withdraw again meant to abandon Texas to the French. To make the missions permanent, it was necessary to extend the sphere of occupation and to make a greater show of strength. To this end and chief in the plans of Spain, was the early establishment of a mission and the erection of a regular presidio on the San Antonio River, to be a half-way post between the remote settlements of the Louisiana frontier and the outlying settlements of Mexico. Father Olivares called attention to the fact that soldiers would be necessary for the protection of his mission. The fiscal not only encouraged an early occupation of Espíritu Santo Bay, but also approved the mission on the San Antonio River, along with a well fortified presidio . . . where ten soldiers of the presidio of Captain Ramón, and from Coahuila, could be permanently assigned for duty. He also recommended that one should be given the rank of Alferez and that Don Martín de Alarcón be sent there with 50 soldiers, suggesting that Capt. Ramón be ordered to return with his soldiers, in case all of the soldiers with Alarcón did not wish to remain permanently on the San Antonio.

After the deliberations of a Junta of War, the viceroy selected Don Martín de Alarcón as a person of authority and zeal in the royal service, to be the commander of the expedition to be sent out for the erection of the proposed missions and presidios. Alarcón was appointed governor of Texas, December 9th, 1716.

Though the mission, *San Antonio de Padua,* founded on the San Antonio River by Father Olivares, had been officially recognized by December of 1716, and though it might have seemed that all preparation for the expedition under Alarcón, had been made by that time, it was not until March of 1718, that final instructions were issued. Alarcón was ordered, among other things, to select a place for a villa and capital, on the banks of the San Antonio, in which there should be erected strong houses of stone for the soldiers' quarters.

The families for the proposed villa, could not cross the swollen streams, so they never arrived. Upon the entry of the expedition to the settlement on the San Antonio, Alarcón discovered that ten families weree already established there; these he considered sufficient for the founding of the villa, which he named *Villa de Béjar.* He founded a regular presidio, and called it the *Presidio de San Antonio de Béjar.* The original San Antonio de Padua mission had its name changed to *San Antonio de Valero,* in honor of the viceroy, the Marquis of Valero. The entire group of settlements was named *San Antonio de los Llanos.* This then, was the beginning of the Spanish occupation of Texas.

Among the prominent families in this early settlement were the Ximenez, Hernández, Barrera, Carvajal, Guerra, Chirino, Valdez, Menchaca, Sosa, Castro, Flores, Maldonado, Galván, Pérez and De La Garza.

Alarcón entered into an open conflict with the missionaries. He resigned his office, and was succeeded by the Marquis of San Miguel de Aguayo, who was appointed Governor of Coahuila and Texas, December 19th, 1719. The Marquis of Aguayo, Don José Ramón de Azlor, was the second son of the first Count of Guara; he was the husband of Ignacia Xaviera Echeverz, heiress of the first Marquis of San Miguel de Aguayo, and the enormous estates of the Urdiñola and López de Lois. With such a formidable fortune at his command, the Marquis of Aguayo was able to recruit and supply a whole military force at his own expense. His expedition into Texas to drive out the French, who were threatening the eastern settlements, and even San Antonio itself, was of far more importance than all others, both in size and results.

The Señor Marqués, who arrived in San Antonio in January of 1722, recognizing that the presidio was exposed to the insults of the Indians, and that it was totally undefended, in addition to being exposed to fire, as had been experienced shortly before, (because of the soldiers living in huts with roofs of straw or hay), undertook the erection of a fortification, with four bastions, 75 varas apart, proportional to the garrison of 54 soldiers, the buildings being made of adobe. "Having had the necessary wood cut for the church, warehouse, and barracks, his Lordship chose a better location than that where the presidio was between the two rivers of San Pedro and San Antonio (although it was necessary to clear the ground, cutting many trees) . . . "

"At the same time his Lordship encouraged the sowing of a large quantity of maize for the provisioning of the presidio, and of the friendly Indians, who came every day to see the Spaniards, by bringing water from the Río de San Pedro which his Lordship did, at his own expense, so as to irrigate two leagues of very fertile land which lie in the angle formed by the *Río de San Pedro* upon entering the San Antonio, below the presidio. It forms a sort of islet, which widens from the place where the presidio is being built. It is 30 varas from the Río de San Pedro and 200 from the San Antonio."

Aguayo did not agree with the ecclesiastical authorities, in that he advised that the presidio should be located on the opposite side of the river from the mission. He said that "it would be better to have not only the barrier afforded by the river, but the wall of the Great Tartary as well, in order the better to keep apart the soldiers and the Indians."

Aguayo also began the fortifications at the Presidio of Our Lady of Loreto, at the site of the original French settlement at La Bahía. He left Domingo Ramón in charge, with 90 men, and returned to San Antonio toward the end of April.

During this interval, the new presidio at San Antonio was "almost completed, and would have been entirely so, had it not been for heavy rains, which prevented work for three weeks, and which dstroyed the adobes which had been built before the departure for La Bahía. Many adobes remained however, and the old ones were repaired, and new ones built. Forty Indians were kept continually at work, and the presidio was finished before the departure of the Marquis, on the 5th of May—"

The Aguayo Expedition "by increasing the military strength of the province of Texas and by the settlement of families," secured to Spain her hold on Texas.

Fernando Pérez de Almazán, one of Aguayo's most trusted officers, was appointed governor of Texas, January 22, 1722. His first official act was the rebuilding of the Presidio of Pilar at the Adaes, which had been destroyed by fire. "In San Antonio he carried out the building of the wall, ramparts, warehouses, officers' and soldiers' houses of the presidio, and this out of his own pocket."

Pérez knew from experience the perfidious character of the Apache, but could not convince the government that action should be taken against them. When the "enemies of the North" murdered Captain Diego Ramón in his very Presidio, the Spaniards and Apaches entered into temporary terms of peace; Captain Nicholas Flores, of the Presidio of San Antonio, is said to have accomplished the Confederacy of the Apaches, and to have gained their friendship for the Spaniards, "all of which was in line with the policy of opening up commercial relations between New Mexico and Texas . . . "

In 1727 Pérez was succeeded by Don Melchor de Media Villa y Ascona. The latter had unfortunate relations with the ecclesiastics; and owing to a formidable league of the Natchez, Apaches and Comanches, which threatened the utter extermination of both the French and the Spaniards, was relieved of his office, and was succeeded by Juan Bustillo Zavallos (1730.) Under the circumstances of the Natchez and their kindred races being so active in the eastern part of the province, Bustillo Zavallos began his administration at the Adaes.

In the meanwhile, acting upon the advice of the Marquis of Aguayo, the king of Spain approved the founding of a villa capital at San Antonio with families from the Canary Islands. San Fernando was thus founded in 1731, under the protection of the Presidio of Bexar.

During the latter part of 1733, the Apaches especially threatened San Antonio. The viceroy ordered the other presidios of the province to be prompt in the execution of the governor's orders, for the mutual defense of Spanish interests. Governor Bustillo Zavallos resigned from office and was succeeded by Captain Manuel Sandoval, who had come to America in 1728, with the appointment of governor of Coahuila. According to *Historia,* 1737, page 532, Sandoval served as Governor and Captain General of the Province of Texas from January 1st, 1734, to September 27th, 1736, on which day Colonel Carlos de Franquis Benitez de Lugo assumed charge. Sandoval was officially installed in office on the 3rd of January, 1734. He began the investigation of the administration of his predecessor on May 14th, and took over the official archives from him on the 29th of the same month. The *residencia* was held at the Presidio of San Antonio de Bexar, as explained in order of June 16th 1734, notifying Bustillo Zavallos of the change from the Adaes. Sandoval had already been present in San Antonio in January, but by August, he had definitely established his residence here. After the termination of the residencia or investigation of the Zavallos administration, on September 8th, Sandoval decided to remain in San Antonio, for in his opinion the principal duty of the governor was to check the audacity of the Indians who infested the vicinity of San Antonio, and to see to it that the new missions and settlements at San Antonio, should prosper. There was nothing of this kind to be accomplished at the Adaes, where there were only presidial soldiers, and where there had not been a single example of Indian attacks. For this reason, then, it was the duty of the governor to reside in the capital, San Antonio. Incessant outrages on the part of the Apaches, convinced the viceroy of the wisdom of this move, and he consequently ordered the governor to continue his residence in San Antonio, particularly as the governor exercised both civil and military authority, and should reside where, aside from a presidio, there was the villa capital of the province.

In spite of the fact that Sandoval reenforced the presidio and defended the community as best he could, he was calumniated before the viceroy by the Captain of the Presidio, and the citizens of the villa, and was relentlessly persecuted by his successor. The outrageous and alarming conduct of Franquis de Lugo, and his false charges against Sandoval, resulted in a special investigation by Antonio Fernández de Jáuregui y Urrutia, governor of Nuevo León, who dispatched Franquis to the presidio on the Río Grande. In the meanwhile the vacancy was filled by Prudencio de Orobio y Basterra (1737-1740).

L ITTLE DEFINITE is recorded in the early manuscripts regarding the governors' place of residence. Sandoval in a speech to the Cabildo of San Fernando, May 9, 1735, enjoined them to better observe the duties of their office. At the adjournment he made "certain explanations distinct and contradictory, one of which was that once he called the *regidores* and other members composing the cabildo in his own house. Among several suggestions he attempted to convince the said cabildo that his house was the one in which the cabildo and the *ayuntamiento* meeting should be held and not in the royal houses . . . " The cabildo disagreed, replying that their meetings should be held in the Royal House of His Majesty, "because it was so ordered by the *ad interim* governor who declared that there was no hall for the ayuntamiento . . . " Sandoval, in proof of what he alleged, called the cabildo's attention to a dispatch and edict of the *residencia* conducted by himself, over the Bustillo administration, "in which it was ordered that it be published in this village and that it be fixed on the houses then serving for the ayuntamiento." He did not however, mention the fact that the judge of the *residencia* had commanded that the customary notices be posted on the doors of the house of the first alcalde, in the absence of an ayuntamiento building, and the house of the first alcalde being a mere jacal, located back of the street, that they be posted on the door of the house of the second alcalde, which was the proper procedure to which the said governor had repeatedly referred.

In 1738, owing to the lack of an ayuntamiento building in San Fernando, official meetings were held, as was the custom, in the houses of the governor and captain general of the province. Notice of the appointment and residencia of Governor Orobio y Basterra was published by ban, April 25, 1738, at about 4: P. M., the most convenient hour when all of the soldiers and inhabitants gathered in the public plaza and usual places, and a signed copy of the *auto* referred to was fixed on the *Cuerpo de Guardia*, on the north side of the Military Plaza, which was adjacent to (*contiguo*) the doors of the residence of the governor.

Captain José de Urrutia, who had become the trusted friend of the Texas Indians during the 17th century, and who had always been a particular advisor to the Marquis of Aguayo, was appointed Captain of the Presidio at San Antonio, July 18, 1733, "to solicit the peace of the Apaches." It is not at all unlikely that his ill feelings tōward Governor Sandoval were partly due, to what might have been the fact, that the governor, outranking him, occupied for a time, the residence of the commander of the presidio, which was located on the west side of the Military Plaza, where most of the officers of the company resided. Urrutia, it is certain, lived in government property just previous to his death, July 16, 1741. The inventory of his estate includes his home in Saltillo, and gives a list of his personal property in San Antonio, mentioning the houses of his residence, but not including them in his estate.

Don Tomás Felipe Winthuisen succeeded Orobio as governor of Texas and held his *residencia* in the Adaes. The customary notice was given in San Antonio, June 16, 1741. Then the king, who had become personally interested in the affairs of Texas, appointed Don Justo Boneo y Morales, and ordered him to draw up a very careful report. His *residencia* over the Winthuisen administration was also held in the Adaes, and made public in San Antonio, January 1, 1744. Boneo died shortly after his arrival in the country of the Adaes. His report was completed by the Auditor, the Marquis of Altamira, whose evidence was strongly in favor of Sandoval. Francisco Garcia Larios was appointed governor, *ad interim,* September 8, 1744, and served until 1748. His *residencia* was held at the Adaes, and published in San Antonio, May 12, 1745.

During the festivities in San Antonio in January 1747, to celebrate the accession of Fernando VI to the Spanish throne, "the governor and the cabildo met in the house which was commonly called the *Palacio*, which was the house in which the governor was supposed to reside . . . " and the parade, at the command of the governor, returned, to the Palace, where the governor resided.

Pedro de Barrio Junco y Espriella, ex-governor of Nuevo León, was appointed governor of Texas in 1748 and served until 1750. He was succeeded by Jacinto de Barrios y Jáuregui, who was in San Antonio in 1751, and who was in command at the Adaes from 1752 to 1754. He exchanged office with Don Angel de Martos y Navarrete, governor of Coahuila, in 1759. Although the *residencia* was held at the Adaes, Navarrete entered upon his duties in San

Antonio. His *visita general* of the province in 1762 throws much light on conditions in Texas at that time. The inspection of the Presidio at San Antonio is interesting. He described the presidio as being "on the north of the Plaza, the buildings being made of stone and mortar, the greater part of which were in ruins. On the south side of the Plaza he said that there was but one jacal. On the west, the house of the Captain with his shop, built of stone or pebbles and mortar, and a very strong edifice; along with other houses, of the same type, occupied by various inhabitants and soldiers. On the east side of the Plaza, he remarked, was only the front (sic) of the church."

Subsequent to the military review of the Marquis of Rubi, which began in Texas in August of 1767, plans for the military reorganization of the forces of the province were drawn up. Lt. Col. Hugo de Oconor was appointed *ad interim* governor, and he assumed official duties toward the middle of 1767. He was an object of fear to the Indians, and in consequence, was called by them the "Red Captain." He preserved peace in the land however, and his disinterested conduct and military policy were causes of the general regret which was expressed upon his return to Mexico in 1770.

The Barón de Ripperdá, who assumed duties as governor in 1770, was particularly active in the execution of the plans of military reorganization. His proposals to construct a fortification in the Presidio of Bexar, capable of mounting from 12 to 14 cannon, was rejected however, as the citizens of the villa were entirely unwilling to cooperate with the presidials. "The presidio of San Antonio was reorganized in accordance with Art. 1, *título* 2, of Royal Regulations, with the Barón Ripperdá, Governor and Commander of the province, as Captain of the Company. His lieutenants were Don Christobal de Córdova and Don Joachin de Orendain . . . the Sergeants, Pedro Granados and Joachin Ruiz; and the Cabos: Antonio Gallardo, Domingo Pérez, Manuel de Urrutia, Manuel Galván, Julián de Arocha and José Antonio Saucedo . . . "

Barón Ripperdá, in his political capacity, resided in the *Casas Reales,* which were located on the east side of the Plaza of the Islanders, in San Fernando (the present northeast corner of Main Plaza and Market Street). He exercised this right in view of the fact that there was no house especially prepared for the residence of the governor and in accordance with custom, in all cities, villas and places where such circumstances existed. It would seem therefore, that the officers' quarters in the presidio were indeed, in a very deplorable condition.

At this time it was ruled that the Captain of the Presidio, having his permanent residence in the presidio, so as to be with his company which garrisoned it, should be considered the same as *castellanos* or *alcaides* of castles and fortresses, and in consequence, should enjoy the civil and criminal jurisdiction conceded to such officers by cited laws in the first instance, though with certain exceptions.

In 1776, Texas, along with other Mexican states, was placed under the military and political government of a commandant-general "directly responsible to the king, and practically independent of the viceroy, the Audiencia of Guadalajara retaining the judicial authority which it had hitherto exercised." The first commandant-general of the Interior Provinces was Theodore de Croix, brother of the viceroy. In 1777, Chihuahua was selected as the seat of the new government of the Interior Provinces. In 1780 Arispe became the capital, but Chihuahua soon again became the official headquarters.

Domingo Cabello was appointed governor of Texas, September 8, 1778, but did not assume duties until November 1, 1778. He was very decided in wishing to reside at the Royal Presidio of San Antonio de Bexar, which he said, was the capital of his principal residence.

In January of 1780, Don José Antonio Curbelo was Lieutenant Governor of the province, residing in San Fernando.

In 1785, the viceregal authority was partially restored over the Interior Provinces, when they were divided into three military districts. Texas was included in the first, under Juan de Ugalde. In 1787 these three military commands were consolidated into two independent jurisdictions, and called the Internal Provinces of the East (which included Texas) and of the West, respectively. Pedro de Nava succeeded Ugalde, but was soon replaced by Ramón Castro. "In 1793 the two commands were reunited into one, independent of the viceroy, as when first established, and Nava was also made independent of the subdelegate of the Real Hacienda... This was the last general change in the system until 1804."

On July 31, 1787, Governor Cabello requested the reconstruction of the building which served as the *Guardia,* and of the *Cuartel,* to which he believed, should have been added, rooms for a prison, and dormitory. His recommendations were approved in Chihuahua, in September of 1786. It was not until 1793, however, during the administration of Governor Muñoz, that the Auditor of War issued the necessary instructions for the actual work. The list of the inhabitants who contributed was signed in the Capitular Hall of San Fernando, October 14, 1793. "The work on the new Cuartel, and the water supply for the plaza was actually commenced. During the winter however, many were of the opinion that it could not be continued during the cold and rain, and for this reason the work was suspended. But all were ready to continue as soon as the winter had passed." In 1801 the *Carcel* (prison) was still useless, and the governor recommended that it should be torn down, "not only because of the weakness of the walls, built with mud instead of mortar, but because of the very poor and ruinous condition of the roof." On August 10th, of this year (1801) the Nolan prisoners were brought to San Antonio; the Americans being imprisoned in the *Casas Reales,* and the Spaniards in the *Cárcel.* So by this date the Cárcel must have been partly repaired. In 1850 the old ruins at the northwest corner of the Military Plaza were converted into the Court House and Jail, and became known as "the Old Bat Cave."

Governor Cabello also resided in the Casa Real, in San Fernando. He refused to even try a case in the *Cuerpo de Guardia* of the presidio, owing to its disgusting condition, and the impossibility of finding any accomodations there.

Cabello was promoted in the service, and was replaced in Texas by Rafael Martínez Pacheco, who was appointed September 18, 1786, assuming duties on December 3rd. Bernardo Bonavia had been appointed governor of Texas on July 8th, "but apparently did not serve." Pacheco was the last of the old governors, for in 1788 the office of governor was ordered suppressed and the province of Texas put under a presidial captain.

At this time (1788) monthly reports were inaugurated regarding military activities in and around San Antonio. Simón de Arocha was the Commander of the Provincial Militia of the Villa of San Fernando. The soldiers' rations, it might be interesting to know, included corn, soap, beans, salt, *Piloncillo* (brown loaf sugar), *chiles* (peppers), and cigarets.

Pacheco, apparently, had some difficulties with church authorities, as well as with the Cabildo of San Fernando. His removal from office was approved October 18, 1790, Manuel Muñoz succeding him, and assuming duties at San Antonio on August 14, 1790. Though Muñoz was at first styled Governor and Captain, he subsequently was called Political and Military Governor. His chief duties were a careful watch for foreign intruders, detailed reports of all foreigners in his jurisdiction, and relations with hostile Indians. He suffered from ill health, and in 1798, it was necessary to appoint Juan Bautista de Elguezabal as his assistant inspector of presidios. Elguezabal assumed duties as *ad interim* governor in 1799; and as governor in 1800; Joseph Irigoyen, apparently appointed in 1798, did not serve.

Antonio Cordero y Bustamante, an expert regarding Indian relations in North Mexico, and governor of Coahuila from 1800 to 1805, was appointed, during the latter year, Military and Political Governor, *ad interim,* of this province of the Texas or the New Philippines, and Commandant of the arms of its coasts and frontiers. He was not long in arriving at Nacogdoches with two companies of troops, and with others to follow, for he realized that if Spain was to hold the province of Texas, it would have to be through military strength. Philip Nolan who had been in San Antonio as early as 1794, had already attempted an Anglo-American invasion of the territory. The claims of the United States to

Texas, in view of the Louisiana Purchase, were indeed alarming to Spanish officials.

"Governor Antonio Cordero married in San Antonio, Gertrudis Pérez, the daughter of Ignacio Pérez (the son of Colonel Joseph Pérez and Paula Granados, Canary Island settlers in San Fernando) and Clemencia Hernández (the daughter of Plácido Hernández, of the 1715 settlers in San Antonio, and Rosalía Montes). There were no children by this marriage. The widow of Governor Cordero married again in 1828, José Cassiano, and they have many descendents in San Antonio today. The Governor's private property, including a beautifully illuminated parchment family history, is now in possession of the Charles P. Smith family, through inheritance from their ancestor, the governor's widow. As Ignacio Pérez purchased the property known today as the Governors' Palace, on the west side of Military Plaza, and made it his homestead, it is very likely that the place was occupied by his relative, the governor, and hence in relatively recent years, has the distinction of being properly called the Governors' Palace.

The following regulation dated October 12, 1805, is of interest: Every foreigner who entered the capital was obliged to present himself at the principal guardia, and if being a distinguished visitor, was expected to present himself at the house of the governor; however, if not being of this category, his second presentation was to be verified at the tribunal of first vote; and from there he was permitted to seek his lodging.

TOWARD the middle of the 18th century, what remained of the original presidio had become surrounded by four streets: Dolorosa on the south, Amargura on the west, Presidio on the north, and Flores on the east.

Along the south side were humble dwellings and the remains of the old ramparts. Brígida Hernández resided there. To her east was the lot of María Luisa Guerrero, widow of Miguel Hernández, who resided however, in her *chamacuero* on the northwest corner of the plaza. To the east of this lot was the corral of the Troop, newly constructed for the horses of the company (1780). Opposite, on the south side of Dolorosa Street, was a lot which belonged to Tomás Travieso. Fernando de Arocha, a soldier, also owned a property facing north on the plaza, "south of which was the house of Diego Menchaca, and another of Plácido Hernández." Diego Menchaca married Rosalía Rodríguez and they inherited their home from her father and grandfrather, Francisco Xavier, and José Antonio Rodríguez, respectively. To the east was the house of Marcelino del Río; and to the west, the house of Alberto Morales. Members of the Flores family possessed both the south corners on either side of Flores Street. In the early part of the 19th century, José María Salinas acquired the Del Río property.

Along the east side of the Military Plaza was the property reserved for the church; the central portion of the ramparts, being selected for the school. To the south was the first two-story house built in San Antonio, that of the Padre, Pedro Fuentes, whose lands extended along the west side of Flores Street, opposite the old Pérez homestead, acquired from the Cabrera family, as far as the gate of the cemetery which faced west. At the southeast corner of Flores and Dolorosa Streets was the Pedro Flores homestead. In 1778 Francisco Menchaca received a grant fronting south on Dolorosa Street, at the corner of Flores Street, bounded by the property of Pedro Flores, and extending to the house of José Pérez, "whose lands touched those destined for the school," and lying east of the grant to Pedro de Fuentes.

The northeast corner of the ramparts was the last private property to be cleared in forming the present plaza in 1889. At the northeast corner of Presidio and Flores Streets (Commerce and North Flores) was the Navarro home, with adobe walls three and one half feet thick. The property of Angel Navarro was acquired from the Ruiz family. To the north was the famous Zambrano Row. The next property adjoining the Navarro on the north, was the *chamacuero* built of good lumber, which Bartolo Seguin acquired from Juan Navarro in 1780.

"The property on the north side of the plazas, facing the street which divided the plazas, was sold in 1716 by Doña Juana de Urrutia, the widow of Ignacio Gonzales de Inclán, to Lieutenant Don Diego Ramón—Marcelino Ramón, the son of Diego Ramón and Teresa Ximenez, came into possession of the property. It was subsequently owned by Matiana Ramón." The next, to the west, was the 1745 grant to Luis Antonio Menchaca; and to his west was the property of Nicolasa Ximenez, wife of Nicolás Flores y Valdez, Captain of the Presidio; parents of María Josefa, who in 1740, as the widow of Miguel Núñez Morillo, received a grant bounded on the south by lands of her mother, east, by lands promised to Alberty López and north, by the so-called *Calle Angosta* (Narrow Street), with the San Pedro to the west.

In 1748 José Montes de Oca sold to Josefa Flores y Valdez, a property along the west side of the Plaza, running back to the creek. On the south was a lot of Francisco Flores, and on the north, one of Josefa Flores, with a street between. The only improvement was a straw cabin (*choza* or *cabaña*) which was already showing its age.

In 1782 the Second Alferez, Marcelo Valdez, received a grant fronting west on the Plaza, running back to the street which separated the property from the San Pedro Creek. "To the north was the dwelling of Juan Francisco Bueno; and to the south, the house of Alberto López."

Cayetano Pérez, an early settler in San Antonio from the Adaes, who married Feliciana Carvajal before 1724, had a stone house facing east on the *Plaza de Armas*. To the north was the jacal of Pedro Minón, with a *Callejón* (alley) between; to the west, the street going to the *Guardia;* and to the south, the jacal of Xavier Zepeda.

The southwest corner of the Plaza and Presidio Street was purchased by María Luisa Guerrero, with the authority of Captain José Menchaca. This was her homestead. Then in 1819 her son-in-law, José Flores, sold the place to Ignacio Pérez for 250 pesos, "at which price his deceased mother had bought it from José Menchaca." The deed also stated that María Luisa Guerrero had sold this property, her dwelling, to said Ignacio Pérez, and had died intestate, without having made a deed of sale.

JOSE ANTONIO MENCHACA, a witness in 1721, was the first of his family in San Antonio. He married a daughter of Captain José de Urrutia and his first wife, Antonia Ramón, and Luis Antonio and José Félix Menchaca were their sons.

Luis Antonio Menchaca was appointed Captain of the Presidio at Bexar in 1763. He also served as *justicia mayor* of the Villa of San Fernando. He was an intimate friend of the Alcalde, Manuel de Carvajal, with whom he had come to San Antonio from Mexico, and through political influence, he was able to claim and receive possession of a portion of the extensive lands which had been occupied by and granted to the Hernández family, from earliest times. By 1773 he had retired from active service, with a pension of 270 pesos per annum. In 1777 he and his brother Félix were accorded military honors, and the use of the official uniform, by decree from Mexico. Several land transactions took place in San Antonio, through verbal contracts with Luis Antonio Menchaca.

Joseph and Luis Mariano were sons of Luis Antonio and his wife Ignacia Núñez Morillo, daughter of Miguel and Josefa Flores.

José Menchaca, in the absence of Francisco Prou, was appointed Alferez of the company in San Antonio (1771). Four years later he was appointed First Lieutenant, upon the retirement of Christobal de Córdova. During the absence of Governor Cabello, he acted as *ad interim* Commander. Luis Antonio and his son José became involved in some irregular transactions in San Antonio, and upon official investigation of what had become of certain goods and effects, José Menchaca was obliged to absent himself from the Presidio of San Antonio. He was subsequently transferred for duty to Coahuila. He retired from service, as Second Lieutenant, in 1794. He married in 1800, and the marriage certificate is the first to appear in the political archives of San Antonio.

Luis Mariano Menchaca inherited the homestead, on the north side of the plaza. His widow, María Concepción de Estrada, sold the property east of the house of Matiana Ramón, in 1817, to Agustín Piernas, who in turn sold it in 1825, to Francisco Maynes, the priest, at which time it was described as being bounded on the east by the houses of José Manuel Núñez. Padre Maynes had been established in San Antonio as first supernumerary chaplain since 1808, and as chaplain proprietor of the Presidial Company, since 1810. He adopted the orphan Jacob Linn, whom he brought from Germany at the age of eight. The Priest's House was left to María de los Santos, for her lifetime, and then to Jacob Linn. Félix Menchaca, who through his mother, was a relative of Manuel Núñez, left him his grant on the north side of the Plaza; Manuel Núñez left the property (three houses east of the Orphan's Asylum of today) to his widow, Brígida Treviño, who died intestate, without issue, and whose estate was taken over by her niece, and only heir, María de Jesús Treviño. She sold the property in 1852, to Jacob Linn for $550.00.

José Menchaca, it would seem, inherited the property on the west side of the Military Plaza, known as the Governors' Palace, from his parents. He sold it on May 17, 1804, to Ignacio Pérez for the sum of 800 pesos, 300 cash, and the balance to cover a note, probably in favor of his brother Luis Mariano. The deed of this sale (1804) describes the property as follows:

A house situated in the village of San Fernando de Bexar and on the west side of Military Plaza; bounded east by the barracks and said Plaza; north by the house of María Luisa Guerrero; south by the house of Andrés del Valle; and west by the San Pedro Creek. Said house had its corresponding depth, west, to the said creek. Said house was composed of one parlor (*sala*), one room, one bedroom (*recámara*), two *zahuanes,* and one kitchen, all of stone, with door and window frames of stone.

José Antonio Pérez and his brother Felipe arrived in San Antonio as single men, with the families from the Canary Islands. José married Paula Granado, daughter of Juan and María Robaina de Bethencourt, all of the Canary Islands. Their son Domingo who married María Concepción de Carvajal, is said to be the ancestor of Antonio Pérez who married Josefa Falcón, whose descendants are well known in San Antonio today. Another son, Ignacio, who was a colonel in the army, married Clemencia Hernández, daughter of Plácido and Rosalía Montes, members of the old families of the presidio. Their son José Ignacio, was the Ignacio Pérez who purchased the Palace property from José Menchaca. He died in 1852, leaving one of the most formidable estates in the community, including twenty-eight different properties. The partition was to the widow, Josefa Cortinas and their children: Ignacio, Jesús, María Trinidad, María Josefa de Linn, Ignacio, the younger, and Concepción. The will of Ignacio Pérez, dated 1849, reads: "I declare that my residence situated on Military Plaza as shown by the deed which I have to the same, will remain for the benefit of my wife, sons and daughter, and in case my children should marry, is will be divided as my will states — 1st, the house which is called of my Aunt María Luisa, with its corresponding depth to the San Pedro Creek, be divided between my sons Jesús and Ignacio, the younger; 2nd, that the small room called of the blessed Virgin, the hall and the kitchen with their corresponding depth to the creek, will be for my daughter Trinidad; 3rd, that the parlor with its corresponding depth, shall be for my daughter María Josefa; 4th, the house which is adjoining the house of José Flores, and four varas more, will be for my daughter Concepción and the parlor will be for the use of my wife, and at her death will be divided in equal parts as is necessary between my daughters."

Concepción Linn, the daughter of Josefa Pérez and Jacob Linn, married Frank T. Walsh. They inherited the properties on the Plaza, and recently sold the old Governors' Palace to the City of San Antonio.

FATHER MARGIL

INDIANS

WHILE the Spanish government, "incited by interest in the Indian tribes northeastward of the Río Grande and by rumors of a threatened French expedition under the Count of Peñalosa" was planning to explore the Gulf coast, "with a view to occupying it and making it the base for an overland route to New Mexico and for the conversion of the provinces of Tagago and Gran Quivira," La Salle landed in Matagorda Bay (1685) and founded his little French colony, protected by fort Saint Louis.

The accounts of this ill-fated visit gave us the first positive notice of the neighboring Indian tribes, whom the French called *Koienkaké, Clamcoéts, Quélancouchis* and *Clamclouches*. The Spaniards learned that the principal tribes of this Karankawan group, not mentioning the numerous petty subdivisions were the Cujanes, Carancaguasas, Guapites or Coapites, Cocos (probably the Coaques or Copoques of Cabeza de Vaca), and Copanes. Their common language was different from their neighbors' farther inland. They were cannibals and represented the lowest grade of native society in all Texas. Additional tribes of the same filiation were the Tups or Tops, Estepisas and Esquein.

On the island not far from the Río Grande, the Malaguitos (probably Apache) were found toward the end of the 18th century; the island was named for them. Around lake San Miguel and on Culebra Island were the Piguiques. Toward the Nueces river were the Manos de Perro. On the shores of Copano bay were the Copanes (who gave their name to the bay), the Guapites and the Inclasco Penas. To the east of the Guadalupe river were the Loguanes. At this time (the end of the 18th century), the Carancaguases inhabited the left bank of the Colorado, near its mouth.

Around Galveston bay, extending to the Netchez, were the *Caux* (French), or Arkokisa, Orcoquiza (Spanish). Further north, on both sides of the Trinity, extending to the Angelina river, were the Bidai, whose tradition claimed that they were the oldest inhabitants of the country where they dwelt. They long kept their independence from the tribes of the Caddo confederacy surrounding them. Still further north, between the upper Brazos and the Trinity, were the Deadose. On the lower Neches and Sabine and to the eastward thereof (in Louisiana) were the Attacapa. These tribes were of somewhat higher advancement than the Karankawa. They were closely associated with one another, and were evidently kin.

T HE Southern group of the great Caddoan linguistic family, comprising the Caddo, Kichai and Wichita, seems, from cultural and other evidence, to have moved eastward from the southwest.

"The advance guard was probably the Caddo proper, who, when first met by the white race, had dwelt so long in the region of the Red River of Louisiana as to regard it as their original home or birthplace." The Caddo group, including the Cadodacho (Kadohadacho, Grand Cado), or Caddo proper, Petit Cado, upper and lower Natchitoches, Adaes, Yatasí, Nassonites, and Natsoos, extended along both banks of Red River, from the lower Natchitoches, in the vicinity Nassonites, above the great bend of the Red River in of Natchitoches city, Louisiana, to the Natsoos and southwestern Arkansas and southeastern Oklahoma.

"West of the Sabine River, on the Angelina and upper Neches, was the compact Hasinai (Asinai, Cenis, Texas) Confederacy, consisting of some ten or more tribes, of which the best known were the Hainai, Nacogdoche, Nebedache, Nasoni, and Nadaco. None of the tribes lived as far west as the Trinity River." The native word *Téjas* or *Texas* means "friends" or "allies" and was used to designate a large group of tribes, not only Caddoan, but others, who were customarily allied against the common enemy, the Apache and Osage.

The Temple in which the *Chenesi* or High Priest kept a perpetual fire, which they worshipped, was situated in the immediate vicinity of the Netchas and Ainais and was common to the two tribes. At a short distance were two little temples, the houses of the *Connicis*, children whom they said, were sent from heaven by their Great Captain, to be consulted when the tribes were in doubt.

There was a second Fire Temple at the Netchas, and a third among the Nacogdoches and Nasonis, to which fire was taken from the first, the veritable *metropoli* of the whole province.

"The Téjas proper inhabited the banks of the *Río de San Pedro*, in a large and well constructed pueblo, of the same name. In 1761, when Fray Gaspar Solís visited the missions, there lived in this village, an Indian woman. who was noted for her authority, and for the respectful consideration she received from the natives. She was called *Canate Adiva*, which means 'Señora Grande,' or 'Señora Principal.' She lived in a big house of many divisions. She was married to five husbands. She was served with extraordinary attention by various servants of both sexes, among whom were not a few *tammas*, and *Conas* (who were *Sacerdotes*—ministers, and *Capitanes*). All of the neighboring nations continually made her presents, and treated her with all reverence, all of which made her a regular queen . . . "

"The Ais tribe, which lay between the Caddo and the Hasinai

groups, though somewhat distinct from either, ethnologists believe, in the main shared the history of the latter."

"As the veil of the unknown was gradually lifted from the district farther north and west, there emerged into view, first on the Canadian River and later on the upper Red, Brazos, and Trinity Rivers, another group of Caddoan tribes, known to the Spaniards of New Mexico as Jumano and to the French as Panipiquet or Panis, but now collectively called by ethnologists the Wichita. Of these tribes the best known to the Spaniards were the Taovayas and Wichita, who habitually lived, after they came distinctly into view, on the upper Brazos, the Wichita, and the upper Red Rivers; and southeast of these, the Tawakoni, the Yscanis, and the Kichai, on the Brazos and the Trinity. During the period between 1770 and 1780 a portion of the Panis-Mahas, or Skidi, disturbed it is believed by the Louisiana cession and the movements of the Osage, came south from the Missouri River and settled with the Taovayas, where they remained until the 19th century."

To the west of these highly cultured Caddoan tribes were the Tonkawan tribes, "occupying a wide range in east-central and northeastern Texas in the middle of the 18th centry." The best known divisions of the group, the Tonkawa, Yojuane, Mayeye, and the highly mixed band of the Yerbipiame, or Erviplame, were usually found above the San Antonio-Adaes *Camino Real*, between the Colorado and Trinity Rivers. "These tribes were wanderers, who planted few crops, but lived upon the buffalo and small game." They were usually ready to join their Caddoan neighbors against the dreaded Apache.

"The greater portion of western Texas was the home first of the Apache . . . and later of the Apache and the Comanche . . . "

T HE *Apache* (a Zuni word meaning "enemy") were one of the chief tribes forming the most southerly group of the Athapascan family. The southern Apache, formerly ranging over southeastern Arizona and southwestern Mexico, included the Gila Apache (Gileños, Mimbreños and Mogollones) and the Querechos or Vaqueros (Mescaleros, Jicarillas, Faraones, Llaneros and the Lipan).

"Till after the opening of the 18th century the Apache tribes, especially the Lipan (who called themselves *Naizhan,* meaning "ours," "our kind") regarded as their own the territory from the upper Nueces and Medina Rivers to the upper Red and Colorado, while their range between summer and winter might cover many hundred miles . . . By the middle of the century the more usual haunts of the Lipan were the districts about the San Sabá River, in west central Texas . . . " continually pressed southward by the Comanche, they were living, in 1777, on both sides of the Rio Grande, "while the Mescalero had retreated to the Bolsón de

Mapimí, in Coahuila." The Carlanes of southwestern Kansas, "the Chilpaines, Palomas, Pelones, Faraones, and Natagés, were all living southeastward from Santa Fé in what are now eastern New Mexico and western Texas."

THE Comanche who called themselves *mimenim* or *num*, ("people"), were of Shoshonean stock of Wyoming. At the beginning of the 18th century they reached New Mexico and the Panhandle country. They crowded the Apache southward destroying their extensive settlements of southwestern Kansas, "and occupying the northern Apache lands themselves." By the middle of th century they occupied the upper Colorado, Brazos, and Red Rivers.

The Comanche was superior to many of the other nations, not only because of their multitude of warriors, and the greater expanse of territory they occupied, but also because of their individual traits. They were particularly noted for their modesty in clothes, hospitality to strangers, who visited them, humanity to captives, who were neither Apaches nor Osages; and lastly for their generosity and their daring valor, which was admirable even in their women. But their wandering life obliged them to become thieves by profession. They lived on dried buffalo meat and Indian bread-root. While engaged in the chase, they had ample opportunity to meet the Apache and learn their numerous and repeated perfidies, as a result of which there was nothing comparable to their hatred for them, or to the cruelty with which they treated them when captives. If the Comanches came to the eastern provinces of New Spain, it was because they were attracted there through their implacable furor in looking for the Lipans and Mescaleros, to seek vengeance for their treachery. The latter in such cases always retreated to the immediate vicinity of the Spanish presidios, and thus gave the Comanches the idea that the Spaniards were their (the Apaches') friends and protectors. The Comanches were so arrogant that one of them alone was quite capable of facing a whole camp of enemies, if unable to secretly avoid it and flee.

A great and distinct group of some seventy cognate tribal or subtribal divisions of Coahuiltecan stock ("now called collectively Coahuiltecan, or Pakwan (Pacoá), from the common language which many of them spoke") ranged from the Sierra Madre to the upper waters of the San Antonio, or to the intermediary tribes (Cantuna, Sana, Emet, Cavas, Tojo, and Toaja) who separated them from the Tonkawan.

The Pakawán were first visited by Cabeza de Vaca who was amused at the different and queer devices of the Pecos-Rio Grande tribes. They had no pots, and in order to cook their beans, *melones* and calabases, filled a gourd with water, and "placed into a fire such stones as easily became heated, and when they were hot to scorch, they took them out with wooden tongs, thrusting them into the water of the gourd, until it boiled," when they put into it, the food they wished to cook, "always taking out the stones as they cooled off, and throwing in hot ones to keep the water steadily boiling."

The Dolores Mission of the Punta ministered to the Pitas and Pajalves (Pasalves). About 40 leagues below, to the east, were the Pauzanes (1727). About 30 leagues to the north of the mission were the numerous Pacoa. Nearby were various other barbarous nations.

The San Juan Bautista Mission on the Rio Grande was founded in 1699 for the Mahuanes and Pachales. Along the Sabinas River were the Mescales and Xarames, who were soon gathered in this mission, with some additional Indians from the Chaguanes (Chahuanes) nation. In 1727 the Mescales were still in the mission, along with some Filixayes and Pastalocos. About 22 leagues south, on the Nueces, were the Pampopas; below them, the Tilixes (Tilijaes); and nearby, the Cacho Postal. Somewhat distant from the mission to the south were also the Patacales.

San Bernardo Mission was founded (in Coahuila in 1703) at the place where there were Ocanes, Canuas, Catuxan, Pazchal and Pamulam Indians; to whom were afterwards added the Pacuaz, Pastaloco, Pappanac, Tuamca, and other of limited number. In 1727 this mission was ministering to the Paguaches, Pastancoyas, Pastalocos, Pachales and Pamasu. About 40 leagues to the south, on the lower San Antonio river, were the Pajalaques. At Carrizo, about 15 leagues below the mission on the Rio Grande, were the Pantascoyas, to whom were joined the Paco. About 18 leagues distant, on the Nueces, were the little Panagues nation. About 60 leagues distant, on the San Antonio, were the Pauzanes. About 15 leagues from the mission were the Paguaches.

Shortly after the middle of the 18th century, these missions on the Rio Grande were ministering to the Pampopas, Tilohayas, Pacholocos and some of the Tuzan nation, of whom there were five Gentiles of the Turan or Carrizo.

The first tribes gathered at the Mission San Francisco de Vizarrón (founded in 1736, ten leagues from the Rio Grande, in Coahuila), were the Piguiques and Pausanes. By 1754 the mission had gathered in Pausane, Pamaque, Piguique, Viayan, Tiligay, and Borrados Indians.

During the first half of the 18th century, the Pamaques and Orejones, speaking more or less the same language, had their habitation and rancherías in the immediate vicinity, between the San Antonio and the Nueces rivers.

FATHER OLIVARES brought new workers for the Rio Grande missions. After visiting the San Juan Bautista Mission, he proceeded to a populous ranchería of Xaranes, and founded the mission *San Francisco Solano,* December 16, 1699, about 40 leagues from the Dolores Mission, in the same Valley of the *Víspera de la Circunción del Señor,* for Xarames Indians, including some Siabanes and Payoguanes, exceeding thirty in number, and some of the Papanac and Siguam tribes.

Owing to an insufficiency of water for three missions, San Francisco Solano was removed, in March of 1705, the *San Ildefonso,* in the Valley of *Encarnación,* about 15 or 16 leagues west of the other two missions, where it was given the name *San Indefonso.* "But this location was in the proximity of the Gavilanes, Ansias, and other hostile Indians, and though the mission was guarded by four or five military, it was only with great hardship and loss of life that anything could be accomplished. There was an abundance of water and wood; commercial relations soon grew up with the surrounding tribes; and the two religious at the mission, along with the few Xarames, the original settlers, were able to attract to the mission over four hundred souls, of the Texocadame (terco dames,) Tiquimamares(tic mamares), Tripasblancas, Xaualines, Piedras Chiquitas (chicas), and many others, including the Juliames, Dedepos and Gavilanes.

In 1708 the cruel Tobosos murdered eight of the peaceful Xarames of the mission, and carried away two of their girls. In consequence, the rest of the Xarame,, refused to remain at the mission. So another locality was decided upon, four leagues from the presidio. Awaiting the necessary formalities for the removal, the missionaries and converts, taking along with them their worldy goods, sought refuge in the San Juan Bautista Mission. The new mission was finally re-established three leagues from San Bernardo, and with its pueblo, was called *San José.*

The missions on the Río Grande continued to flourish until 1718, when Father Olivares transferred his mission San José (San Francisco Solano) to San Antonio and merged it with his mission *San Antonio de Padua,* already established at that place, calling the new mission *San Antonio de Valero.*

THE Payaya were one of the most important of the Coahuiltecan tribes. Their village, Yanaguana, was first called *"San Antonio de Padua"* by the Spaniards, when Father Manzanet, in 1691, erected a cross and altar there, and through a Pacpul interpreter, explained the Christian doctrine, and after mass distributed rosaries, gaining the good will of the Payaya chief by the gift of a horse. This was at the site of present San Antonio.

The Payaya were at San Francisco Solano Mission as early as 1706.

THE Olivares-Espinosa-Aguirre Expedition of 1709 found the Payaya ranchería " in a clearing along" the east bank of the Medina. Upon crossing this stream a second time, at a bend further east, they found the Pampoa ranchería, where they took an Indian on horseback as a guide, and where they were accompanied by twelve of the Pampoa on foot. The expedition forded the León creek about a gunshot from where General Gregorio Salinas Varona (governor of Coahuila, 1692-1697, and of Nuevo León, 1705-1707) crossed it, and on the other side of a large plain and mesquite flat, and some holm-oak groves, they came to "an irrigation ditch, bordered by many trees." Here, Father Espinosa observed, was water enough to supply a town. "It was full of taps or sluices of water, the earth being terraced." This they named *Agua de San Pedro* (San Pedro Creek), April 13th 1709, remarking that the river formed by the spring, "could supply not only a village but a city." At this site was a populous ranchería of Siupan, Chaulaames and some Sigames Indians, numbering about 500 in all.

This expedition was disappointed in not meeting "the Asinai Indians, commonly called Tejas" on the Colorado, whom they had hoped to induce to move to the Rio Grande missions. With the uncertainity of their whereabouts; not having planned to stay any longer; the Captain not having instructions to go farther eastward, and having been told by all who knew him, that the chief of the Tejas, Bernardino, a very crafty Indian who had lived among the Spaniards, was very adverse to all matters of faith, never having been made to live like a Christian, and that he had escaped from the mission on the Rio Grande with some Indian women who had been left there, the expedition decided not to proced any farther.

When they recrossed the San Antonio (April 23rd) on the return, they did not find the people they had left there, because they had moved down the river. When approaching the Medina, westward, the Spaniards were met by the Pampoa Indians who came out to see them, as well as by the Captain of the Paxti nation.

This multitude of Coahuiltecan tribes and subtribes were docile and weak; and according to Bolton, were the only exception to the Karankawans in representing the lowest grade of native society in all Texas. The Pakawá were "without agriculture or fixed habitation, but roving from place to place, subsisting upon game and the wild fruits of the mesquite, pecan, and cactus, dwelling under temporary shelters of brushwood and grass thatch, and with very little tribal cohesion or organization." They were probably not cannibals; and while inconstant, "seem to have been of unwarlike and generally friendly disposition."

"These were the tribes or bands that furnished the bulk of the neophytes for the San Antonio and Rio Grande missions. By the middle of the 18th century many of the bands had become much reduced or had entirely disappeared, exhausted by smallpox, measles, and the drain made by the missions. Soon after this date, the Lipan, the great Apache division of whom the Coahuiltecan tribes stood in mortal dread, crowded southward into the original territory of the Coahuiltecos and forced the survivors to the coast," from whence (after 1760) they "continued to furnish a small supply of material for the languishing missions, but, being peaceful and having practically no fighting strength, they were of little political interest."

INLAND from the Karankawa, on either side of the lower Guadalupe River, lived the Xaraname, Tamique, and smaller kindred bands. As they occupied the border land between four great stocks, the Coahuiltecan, Karankawan, Bidai-Arkokisa, and Tonkawan, it is hard to say to which of these, if any, they belonged. It is believed, however, that they spoke a language distinct from that of the Kakankawa, their nearest neighbors on the south. It may possibly be significant in this connection that when about 1760 the Xaraname apostatized and left their mission they joined the Tonkawa. Perhaps, however, the affinity, which directed them thither, was only one of customs and not of language or race."

FATHER Francisco Hidalgo, who had worked at the Nabedache missions before their desertion in 1693, and who had made various unsuccessful efforts (after 1700) to obtain permission to return to his former charge," finally, in 1711 and 1712, feeling assured that if he could but give an actual demonstration to his government and college of the danger from the French, he would be sure of receiving the coveted permission, "turned for aid first to the missionaries and then to the secular authorities of Louisiana." His appeal to the missionaries which came to Governor Cadillac's attention in 1713, arrived at a most opportune time. In consequence of Crozat's grant of 1712, for a fifteen-year monopoly of the trade of all the country south of the Illinois and between the Spanish and the English colonies, Louis Juchereau de Saint Denis was sent in 1713 to the Natchitoches tribe to open up trade with the Indians. With Father Hidalgo's letter as a pretext, he was soon on his way to the Rio Grande to establish an overland commerce with Mexico. He arrived at San Juan Bautista on July 19th, 1714. Finding that Father Hidalgo, to whom he had already addressed a letter, was at Querétaro he dispatched a second letter, to him at that place. St. Denis was arrested and sent to Mexico City where an investigation was made of his proceedings.

"Alarmed by what they learned from Saint Denis' deposition lest the French should gain dominion over the eastern tribes and their territory, and pass beyond to monopolize the trade and discover the mines of Mexico, the authorities of Mexico organized an expedition designed to contest the advance of the French, as well as to carry out the long cherished plans of Father Hidalgo. Saint Denis, who perhaps regarded this step as the very one to help on his superior's plans for trade, and who, to quote Arricivita, 'bore in his person that character which marks honorable men and makes it impossible to doubt their word,' was plausible enough to overcome mistrust of his own designs and to get himself appointed guide for the expedition. The enterprise, therefore, was put in charge of Domingo Ramón, for the civil and military, and Fathers Margil and Espinosa, for the religious work, with St. Denis as *cabo comboyador.*" It was owing to the zeal of Father Margil, that this, the Zacatecan College, joined with the Queretaran College, on this important mission.

When this expedition reached the waters of the San Pedro, Father Espinosa observed (May, 1716), the sufficiency for a mission, while the San Antonio river was very desirable for settlement, owing to its "pleasantness, location, abundance of water, and multitude of fish." The region was then overgrown with "very tall nopals, poplars, elms, grapevines, black mulberry trees, laurels, strawberry vines (sic) and genuine fan-palms," as well as with "a great deal of flax and wild hemp, and abundance of maiden-hair fern and many medicinal herbs."

Between the Colorado and Trinity rivers, the Ramón Expedition was guided by a Payaya Indian.

This expedition began a new frontier policy, It established (1716) four missions (San Francisco, Conception, Guadalupe and San José) nearer the frontier than the original San Francisco; while Father Margil established, in the following spring of 1717, two more missions (Dolores and San Miguel) farther eastward for the Ais and the Adaes tribes, "the latter establishment being well across the Sabine in what is now Louisiana and only seven leagues from the French post of Natchitoches." This expedition also established the Presidio of *Dolores* or *de los Téxas*, on the Angelina river. "The three easternmost missions were under the Zacatecas friers, the other under those from Querétaro."

The Texas corn crop failed. The missionaries suffered great privations, living on herbs and nuts, with occasional bits of meat given them by their Indians. In response to Ramón's requests for aid, the Marquis of Valero, who had assumed the duties of viceroy (August 16, 1716), sent not only food stuffs but soldiers and mechanics as well. "But when the slow moving expedition reached Trinity River in December, 1717, they found it so swollen that they were unable to cross it. The carriers of the supplies made a caché at Río de las Cargas, and the missionaries before returning dispatched letters by Indian hunters to inform the Fathers among the Asinais of what had befallen them, with information as to the place of the caché. It was not, however, till the following July that tidings of the proximity of the needed provisions reached the famishing missionaries."

It now became necessary for the Spaniards to select a district for a permanent settlement. The eastern frontier they soon larned, was too exposed to the enemy; the coast country was inhabited by decidedly hostile savages; so to be a half-way station, near the Rio Grande, and on the route from La Bahía (where provisions were received from Veracruz), it was decided that the headquarters of the San Antonio and San Pedro, so frequently approved for a settlement, should be the site for the first of a line of presidios extending to the Tejas mission.

THE FORT OF SAN ANTONIO DE VALERO (ALAMO)

View from top of Veramendi House. Drawing done seven years before the Fall of the Alamo. Formerly in Berlandier Collection. From reproduction in S. A. Express.

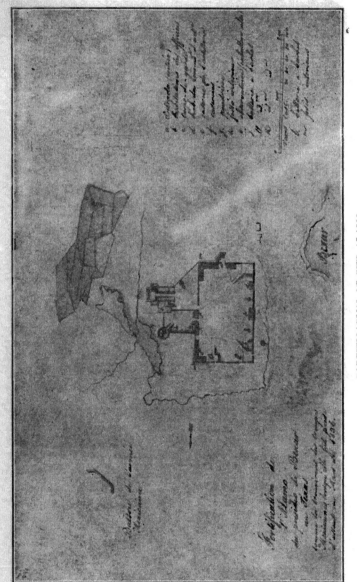

FORTIFICATION OF THE ALAMO

As it was found by the Mexican troops at the time of the attack and fall, in 1836.   Courtesy of Yale University.

MISSIONS

In the meanwhile, through the care and diligence of the experienced veteran, Father Antonio San Buenaventura y Olivares, a mission had already come into existence on the banks of the San Antonio de Padue river. Father Olivares who was called before the viceroy, presented written plans for the founding of the mission, which he called *San Antonio de Padua*. He recommended and requested a military guard, as well as supplies, and presents for the Indians. He also asked that the San Francisco Solano mission be transferred from the Rio Grande to his San Antonio mission.

With the Fiscal's approval, a Junta of War, called on December 2, 1716, authorized the mission and presidio on the San Antonio; the mission being officially recognized as already existing on December 7, 1716.

The commander of the expedition to be sent out for the official founding of the mission and presidio was to be a person of authority and zeal in the royal service, as well as in the salvation of souls, experienced in dealing with the Indians, and liberal and kind in his treatment of them. The viceroy announced as his selection for this service, Don Martín de Alarcón, a soldier of distinguished service in Old and New Spain, and appointed him governor of Coahuila (August 5th) and governor of Texas and the New Philippines on December 9th, 1716, with special instructions to look after colonization.

Father Olivares was promptly appointed founder and missionary for the mission on the San Antonio. He knew the different Indians, and it was most likely that with proper support he would be able to gather in the surrounding tribes for the service of God and of His Catholic Majestic. He had already located an admirable site for the founding of the mission, where four of the Christianized Xarame Indians were established in jacales, on the banks of the San Antonio river.

Alarcón's Expedition arrived at San Antonio in March of 1718. The San Antonio de Padua mission was now called *San Antonio de Valero*, in honor of the viceroy. The San Francisco Solano mission was officially merged with it, on May 1, 1718. The *Presidio de San Antonio de Béxar* was officially founded. Though the families intended for the new villa did not arrive with the expedition, on account of the high water in the Rio Grande, the ten soldiers with their families, most of whom had come with the Ramón Expedition, and who were already at the San Antonio de Padua mission, were considered by Alarcón, as sufficient for the founding of a villa, which he called *Villa de Béjar*. The entire group of settlements was called *San Antonio de los Llanos*.

It is interesting to note that the Payaya chief to whom Father Manzanet had given his horse in the 17th century, and his tribesmen, were present at the ceremonies of 1718.

The Xarame and Payaya, speaking more or less the same language, were prompt in entering the mission. The Sanes and Vanos were also among those of earliest date.

According to Alarcón's own statement, he departed from the Villa de Bejar on the 5th of September, 1718, the villa having already been formed with ten families which he left sufficiently guarded by soldiers. What was particularly needed were missionaries as Father Olivares was all alone, with many Indians, none of the other missionaries wishing to accompany him, in spite of the fact that the King had made allowance for three of them.

Father Olivares remained at his new mission, San Antonio de Valero, for a year, "laboring to gain the neighboring Indians, and preparing the foundation of the future town. Unfortunately, while one day crossing a rude bridge, his horse broke through and threw the missionary, causing a fracture of his leg. Father Peter Muñoz hearing of his mishap, hastened from the Rio Grande to support his place and give him the necessary attention. When Father Olivares recovered he transferred his mission from its original site to one on the opposite side of the river, which it maintained for years." Here (on the east side of the river), it consisted of a small stone tower used as a granary, and several jacales, which served as church and living quarters.

In 1724 a furious hurricane destroyed the primitive mission. In consequence, a more convenient site was chosen, about two gun-shots away (the site of present Alamo Plaza).

By 1727 the mission had three cells of very good proportions, a gallery and another cell, all of stone and adobe; the convent was under construction. There was also an irrigation system which watered the fields. Up to this time (1727) no stone church had been erected, but the necessary materials for one were collected and work was to begin immediately. The new edifice was to be spacious and to have a good door, with appropriate decorations.

The first ten years of the existence of this mission were spent mainly in gathering the Xarami Indians who had come from the San José (San Francisco Solano) mission, and who had scattered to the wilds in the vicinity of the San Antonio river. Others were also invited to join the mission: Yerebipiamos, Muruabes, and Paguaches. In 1727 there were 70 families of Indians in the mission, of three nations: the Xarames, Payayas and Yerebipianos, totalling 273 souls of both sexes, of whom only 164 were faithful Christians. At an earlier date there had been more Indians in the mission, but death had claimed many of them, the records showing the death of 127 baptised adults, and 30 baptized infants. In the immediate vicinity of San Antonio there were the Sanas, numbering about 200, with whom the Mayeye had gathered, numbering about 200. Their headquarters were on the Brazos. The Rancheria Grande, above the Trinity, at a place called *Navisi*, was made up of barbarous nations, including some apostates who had fled the missions and sought refuge there.

During the 30's, a terrible epidemic reduced the mission to 184 souls. But owing to the successful conversions of Tacamanes Indians, the total population in 1740, amounted to 261.

The corner stone of the new church was placed on May 8, 1744, during the administration of Fray Mariano Francisco de los Dolores.

The Indian pueblo consisted of two rows of adobe and thatched houses, separated by a ditch, and surrounded by a wall. The monastery, though small, contained upper cells, where the missionaries lived. The weaving room was used by the women and old men in making their cloth, blankets and covers from the wool and cotton produced on the mission lands.

Some twenty years later (1761) the convent was in a flourishing condition, with two stories of arcaded cloisters. The porter's lodge (*porteria*), refectory, kitchen and offices, were all properly furnished and religiously adorned. The weaving room was in the second patio, along with two store rooms well supplied with wool, cotton, and tools. The church tower was now completed, though the sacristy had fallen in, owing to the poor work of the inexperienced builder. During the reconstruction, religious services were being held in the room, 35 varas long, originally built for the granary.

A ditch planted with willows and fruit trees flowed through the spacious plaza; a well had also been dug (in the convent, as a precaution in case of an attack from the Indians who might cut off the ditch). The arched portales around the plaza were particularly attractive. The tower was at the main entrance.

President Father Dolores reported in 1762 that the total population of San Antonio de Valero amounted to 275 Xarames, Payayas, Zanas, Yprandes, Cocos, Tojos, and Carancaguases, emphasizing the fact that particular care was being given to the conversion of the latter.

In 1767 the College of Querétaro assumed the conduct of the missions in Sonora, or Pimería Alta and Pimería Baja (Arizona), which were left vacant upon the expulsion of the Jesuits in that year. When Rubio's proposals to abandon the "imaginary" possessions of Spain beyond San Antonio were adopted in the "New Regulation of Presidios" which called for the strengthening of San Antonio's defences, and for the increase of the population in its population in its neighborhood, the Queretarans gave up their missions in Texas, in 1772 to the Zacatecans so as to better conduct their work in Pimería Alta. With this supremacy of the Zacatecans, the old Queretaran missions began to decline.

The Indians at San Antonio de Valero so decreased that it was necessary to abandon the weaving rooms; and at the beginning of 1778, there were hardly enough Indians to do the work in the field. Some people then went to the Commandant General, Caballero de Croix, and informed him of this scarcity of Indians, requesting that the lands be turned over to the refugees from the abandoned Adaes settlement, who were without domicile, and without even a small piece of land to raise their crops. Some of the *Adaeseños* who had petitioned the governor (October, 1773), to be permitted to settle at Los Ais, remained at Bexar.

His excellency, after considerable reflection, found it convenient to provide that the few Indians of the Valero mission be distributed among the wandering inhabitants of the depopulated Presidio of the Adaes. The original settlement at the Adaes had languished on, until 1790, when it was definitely broken up and deserted, the inhabitants removing to San Antonio.

In 1793 the Valero mission records were transferred to the archives of the Villa of San Fernando and Presidio of San Antonio de Bexar, when the pueblo was aggregated to the curacy of Bexar. Governor Muñoz reported, on May 27, 1793, that he had complied with the viceroy's instructions (of January 9, 1793); that he had divided the lands of the former mission as well as the oxen, cows, tools and seed, among the inhabitants of the abandoned presidio of the Adaes, the Indians of the mission, and those who had aided.

These lands, divided among the 40 Adaeseños, the mission Indians, and the 16 San Antonio families, were on the east bank of the river, north of the mission, including the *suertes* between the mission ditch and the river, and were later called "the *Labor* of the *Adaeseños*."

The church of the mission had never been finished. It was of Tuscan (rough) workmanship with transepts. The vaults corresponding to the arches were crestshaped. The vault of the *Previsterio* was finished with its tower arch, and the other three were closed without vaults, and ready to receive the dome. The baptistry was finished. The principal door of the church was described as particularly beautiful, of Tuscan workmanship, with four niches, two of which were ornamented with stone images of San Francisco and Santo Domingo.

In 1796 there was a decrease of population in the pueblo, of 36 from the total of 158, of the previous year. In 1797 there were 139.

The mission church was again used for religious services when the Flying Company of San Carlos de Parras, originally from the Pueblo de San José y Santiago del Alamo, Mexico, was stationed at San Antonio, and quartered in the mission property. As a protection against Indian attacks, they erected barracks along the south side and inside of the old enclosure.

In abbreviation, the early records of this company refer to the "Pueblo del Alamo." When the first baptism in the military chapel or the old mission church was recorded (1803), the place was referred to as "the Alamo."

On April 1, 1812, the company turned their records over to the parish church of San Fernando, and subsequently evacuated the place. When the Republican army of the North took San Antonio (April 1, 1813), they made their headquarters in the Alamo. Then when the Royalists reconquered the place (August 20, 1813), the Company of the Alamo returned and remained here until late in th 20's.

"When San Antonio fell into the hands of the Texans in December of 1835, the Mexicans lost their last foot hold in Texas and San Antonio became 'the key to the situation,' a point to be held at all hazards, because if the Mexicans could re-take and hold it, they could more easily oppose the American colonies. Travis certainly appreciated this fact when he so boldly took his stand with a mere handful of compatriots against the Mexican army. When Santa Anna marched into San Antonio on the afternoon of February 23rd, 1836, the Texas guard retired into the Alamo which had already been provided as a means of defense, as Colonel Travis had anticipated an attack. Santa Anna immediately demanded a surrender, threatening however, to put the garrison to the sword should they refuse. The Americans answered the summons with a cannon shot and their flag remained waving proudly from the walls."

The capture of the Alamo by the Mexicans under Santa Anna on the 6th of March of 1836, and the slaughter of its garrison of 183 men, spread consternation throughout the land. Here the gallant few, throwing themselves between the enemy and the settlements, fell the chosen sacrifice to Texas freedom. Their detaining the enemy enabled Texas to rcuperate her energies; " it enabled her to assemble upon the Colorado that gallant band, which but for Houston would there have fought and beat the enemy, and which eventually triumphed upon the plains of San Jacinto and rolled back the tide of war upon the ruthless invader."

SAN JOSE MISSION

Wood cut, 1857. Owing to the architectural beauty of San Jose Mission it is probably
the most profusely illustrated of all the Texas missions.

SAN JOSE DE SAN MIGUEL DE AGUAYO

THE Ramón Expedition (1716) was answered by the French of Louisiana in an increase of their garrison at Natchitoches. They were prepared to resist any attempt that the Spaniards might make to cross Red River. It is very evident that it was their policy, however, to encourage Spanish progress, as a means of promoting trade over the border, rather than to drive them from the establishments they had already made. "But the Spaniards on the frontier, not fully understanding this policy and lacking the French zeal for trade, felt anything but safe, while the French local authorities could not consistently maintain it, as was shown in 1719. When in that year war broke out in Europe between Spain and France, it spread at once to the colonies. Pensacola was promptly captured by the French of Mobile, and, contrary to the desires of the trading interests, orders were given to Blondel, the commandant at Natchitoches, to drive the Spaniards from Texas. In the execution of this command Blondel went in person to Los Adaes and arrested the only Spaniards who were there at the time and carried off the ornaments of the mission church. One of the prisoners, escaping, carried the news to Nacogdoches and the presidio on the Angelina, whereupon the missionaries and the garrison retreated to San Antonio, fearing, as they said, an attack by the French and Indians combined. As a punishment for their allegiance to the Spaniards, we are told, after the retreat of the latter the Adaes tribe were removed from their lands by the French and treated as enemies. After peace had been restored Blondel was reprimanded by La Harpe, representative of the Company of the Indies, now proprietor of the colony, for his descent upon Los Adaes, and was required by him to apologize, though Blondel insisted, on good grounds, that in his advance upon the mission he had only obeyed orders."

The Marqués de Aguayo, who assumed the government after Alarcón's resignation, was sent by the viceroy to restore the Spanish frontier. "He reestablished the presidio of *Nuestra Señora de los Dolores*, or '*Téxas*,' and the six abandoned missions. More important still, he planted a new presidio in the Adaes tribe beside the mission of San Miguel. This establishment, which for half a century remained the capital of Texas, was on the site of the present Robeline, Louisiana. To prevent the French from reoccupying the Bay of Espíritu Santo (Matagorda Bay), as well as to furnish a base of communications with Mexico by water, he also erected, in 1722, a presidio and a mission on the site of La Salle's fort, among the Karankawan tribes . . . " And as has already been noted, "*The Señor Marqués*, who arrived in San Antonio in January of 1722 . . . undertook the erection of a fortification, with four bastions . . . the buildings being made of adobe

. . . His Lordship chose a better location than that where the presidio was between the two rivers of San Pedro and San Antonio."

Among the missionaries seeking refuge in San Antonio was Father Margil, who while enjoying the hospitality of the Queretaran Mission of San Antonio de Valero, was ambitious to found a mission of his own, which would serve the Zacatecans, and make them independent of the Queretarans. To this end he addressed the new governor, Aguayo (December 26, 1719), calling attention to the fact that three captains of the Pampoas Indias had already come to the Zacatecan fathers, to request a mission, as they had seen how corn was grown at the Valero Mission, and they too wished to cultivate and gather much of it. Father Margil concluded that aside from the necessary supplies for the Indians, little in the way of ornaments would be necessary for the proposed mission, as the Zacatecans already had an image of San Joseph, bequeathed them on the condition that it be used in the founding of a mission to be named in honor of that saint. Father Margil added however, that the new mission should be called *San José de San Miguel de Aguayo*, not overlooking this delicate attention to the marquis.

"On January 22nd, 1720, after receiving notice from all the surrounding places of the said *villa* (San Antonio) that there were many docile and friendly nations desirous of being shown the evangelic light (the nearest and first being the Pampoas, who numbered about 200), the marquis of Aguayo commissioned his Lieutenant General, Captain Juan Valdez, in the name of the king, and of himself, as Governor and Captain General of the Province of Coahuila, Nueva Estremadura and of Texas of the New Phillipines, to select a site which would seem most convenient and where there was abundant water and fertile land for fields and pasturage of every kind, and found on it a mission with the name of *San José de San Miguel de Aguayo,* and that possession of the same be given the Most Rev. Father Fray Antonio Margil de Jesús, President of said Preeching Missionary Fathers, with the ceremonies provided by law, and that the appropriate governors and officers be appointed from the sons so congregated."

On February 23, 1720, Captain Juan Valdez reported to Aguayo, that with the commission sent him from Monclova, and in the name of His Majesty, and of the Marquis of Aguayo, he had given possession to the Pampoas, the Pastias and the Suliajames . . . Captain Lorenzo García acting as interpreter. Those present were Fr. Antonio de San Buenaventura Olivares, of the mission of San Antonio de Valero, Fr. Marjil de Jesús, as Prelate, and others: fathers. missionaries, including Fr. Joseph Guerra, and soldiers, with the Alferez, Nicolás Flores y Valdez.

The party arrived at the point where water was taken from the San Antonio river for irrigation purposes, where they found the Rev. Fathers Fr. Agustín Patrón and Fr. Miguel Núñez de Haro, in a jacal, accompanied by some soldiers who were posted there at the orders of Captain Alonzo de Cárdenas. The entire party, including the Indian captains, inspected the lands, pasturages and the river which was near, and as there was much wood and many poplars with open spaces for the cattle to graze, it seemed the best place for the location of the church and pueblo. A high spot was chosen for the building. Inquiry was made as to the distance from the mission of San Antonio de Valero, and the reply was about three leagues. Here possession was then given. They all shook hands with the Indian Chiefs. Then the Indians were instructed through the interpreter, as to their duties in tilling the soil, and in teaching their children to do the same, as well as to worship the Lord. The water rights were also granted, all of which was quietly accepted, without any contradiction whatever; weeds were pulled, stones thrown, branches cut from the hill side, and all of the customary acts of possession were gone through with, and all were content with the lands and water. The pueblo was founded nearby, and called *San José de San Miguel de Aguayo de Buena Vista,* in the name of His Majesty. Captain Valdez stated that he selected a site for the church, with ample rights for the cemetery, and all that was customary for the convent, hospital and for the Royal Houses and barracks, and all other necessities. The plaza was one hundred and twenty varas square, and the houses were constructed in the customary manner, and the streets as well. So the settlement should grow, and prosper, they built houses and huts, and raised Spanish chickens and *chachalacas (Gallinas de la tierra).*

In the name of His Majesty, Juan, the Captain of the Pampoas, was appointed Governor; Nicolás, the Captain of the Suliajames, was appointed *Alcalde;* and Alonzo, Captain of the Pastias, was appointed *Alguacil.* Francisco, of the Pampopa nation, and Antonio, of the Suliajame nation were appointed *regidores.*

In due time, the auto of foundation was transmitted to Monclova. The Marquis of Aguayo acknowledged the founding of the mission from Monclova, March 13, 1720.

The Rev. Fathers Fr. Miguel Núñez and Fr. Agustín Patrón and the said soldiers under orders of Captain Alonzo de Cárdenas, were left in charge of the mission and pueblo.

This was the beginning of a monument, which in time, outshone all others in solitary grandeur, a missionary masterpiece of art and beauty, unrivalled in all New Spain. It heralded the approach of the benefactor, and his expedition, "with the strongest military force that had ever yet entered Texas."

By May of 1768, there were recorded in the mission, 1054 baptisms, 287 marriages, and 359 burials. There remained at the mission (1768) about 350 men, "advanced in years, learning and experience;" of whom about 110 were skilled in managing arms, 45 armed with rifles, and 65 with bows and arrows, lances and other arms. Along with the original Indians of the mission, (Pampoas or Pampopas, Mesquites and Pastias) there had gathered Camamas, (Tacames), Canos, (Cannas), Aguastallas and Xaunaes (Xaunaos). The missionaries were making particular attempts to attract the faithless coast tribes.

All of the Indians were well trained in civilized customs and christianity. All of them spoke Spanish, except those who came in from the wilds when grown, and refused to become tamed. Most of them were skilled in playing the guitar, violin or harp. Their voices were sonorous. On Saturdays, each 19th day, and the feast days of Christ and Holy Mary, they took out their rosaries, and sang in four voices (soprano, alto, tenor and bass), accompanied by the corresponding instruments. It was glorious to hear them. All of the Indians, both men and women, knew how to sing and dance after the manner of the white people from abroad, and perhaps with even more skill and beauty. They were all decently dressed, each having two suits, one for work days, and the other, better one, for feast days. The Indians were not ugly; their women were comely and very graceful; though an occasional one was surly and lazy.

The Indian men occupied themselves with the work that was to be done. The old men made arrows for the soldiers. The young women spun and untangled the wool, and sewed. The old women spent their time fishing to supply the table for the holy fathers. The boys and girls attended school, and said their prayers in turn.

In spite of the mission culture, the Indians following their natural inclinations, would take advantage of the friar's carelessness, and flee to the wilds to participate in the native *mitotes* (dances) along with the pagan Indians. This was carefully watched for however, and those caught so trespassing, were severely punished for their guilt.

They all had their beds in high places with their large warm blankets of cotton and wool, woven in the work-shop of the mission, their sheets and covers, and buffalo hides for mattresses.

In short, the Indians of San José Mission were so well trained in civilized life and so cultured that the Indians from outside, who were already among the white people, would require a long time to become as highly advanced.

The lines of the mission were those of a perfect square. The four fronts of buildings which formed the walls were 220 varas long, each having a similar entrance. There were the little dwellings of the Indians, four varas deep and five or six varas long. In each was a kitchen and chimney, and look holes which fell on the outside for defensive purposes.

Some of the closed arches of the portals of the dwellings of the ministers were of fair size. They were sufficient for all of the necessary offices.

The church of San José Mission was just beginning to be built. It was to be of stone and lime, with arches 50 varas long and 10 varas wide in its transept. The first stones were laid by the Governor and Captain General of the Province of Texas, Don Hugo O'Connor, and the inspector for the College of Zacatecas, Father Fray Gaspar José de Solís, who blessed the new structure (March 19, 1768).

There was an arched granary of stone and lime, of three vaults; a weaving room where they made woolen blankets, and very good cotton and woolen cloth in quantity; a carpenter shop, an iron shop, and a tailor shop. There was also a furnace for burning lime and brick. "In 1781 its tanneries and other manufactories were held as an example for the other settlements, which De Croix hoped would be interested in the promotion of such enterprises."

The irrigation ditch was so large and had so much water in it that it looked like a small river. It contained a great number of fish. In the fields, which were fenced in for more than a league, they raised such an abundance of corn, brown beans, lentils, melons, water-melons, peaches, sweet potatoes. Irish potatoes, and sugar cane, that they were able to supply the other missions, as well as the Presidios of San Antonio, La Bahía, San Sabá, Orcoquisac and Los Adaes. In the garden they raised all kinds of vegetables, and many fruits, particularly peaches. of which individual ones weighed as much as a pound, from time to time. The olives were superior to those of France.

This mission had a ranch of from 10 to 12 leagues, called *Atascoso*, where there were "about ten droves of mares, four droves of burros, about thirty pair, about 1500 yoke of oxen for plowing, and about 5000 head of sheep and goats." They also had all the necessary tools and implements.

Everything at this mission was done by its own Indians who were very industrious workers and very skillful in everything.

With the decline of the original Queretaran missions, San José (of the Zacatecas College) became "the center of the Texas missions and residence of the president or Superior." By 1778, a rather low bulwark, for defense, was over each of the four entrances. In the concave or inside of each entrance were openings on each side, which corresponded to the lateral habitations, where the neophytes lived in greater confidence, for if their enemies should attack the entrances with their hatches, they could fire upon them from cover. In the west line of rooms, in front of the church, was a fifth entrance, which was defended with its gateway, which was the only one left open each day, for the service. In front of this entrance was an extensive cleared space, to prevent the enemy's approach under cover.

In January of 1778, a good part of the vaulted roof of the church had not yet been finished. Some two or three years later however, the entire church edifice was being completed. There were three arches and one beautiful nave, 50 varas long, by 10 varas wide, with the corresponding transept. The dome was very beautiful, though charged with "useless" mouldings. The proportions were good. The stone used, which came from the Conception quarries, was coarse-grained, sandy, and granitic, rough, porous, and light, and when mixed with lime, became solid, and useful as the *tesontle* of Mexico.

The main entrance was very costly, on account of the statues and "trifling" mouldings with which it was charged, which, in Morfi's opinion, detracted greatly from its beauty. In the center of this entrance, and over the principal door was a balcony, which gave a great air of majesty to the structure. The entrance to the balcony was a sexagonal window, instead of the usual door.

It was hard to believe that in such a remote region, there had been such good artists, and it was more to be admired, as all the work had been done by the children of the mission.

The sacristy, where divine service was temporarily held, was a large room of one vault with good light, and very gay. Its decorations inspired devotion in whoever saw it. It was rich in sacred vessels and ornaments. Its door opened on the little cloister or corredor of the two-storied convent.

The quarry of this mission was near the main entrance to the patio. The soft chalky stone could be planed the same as soft wood, received the polish of marble, and when exposed to the air became hard. The railing of the convent staircase (a spiral in perfect balance) and a statue in its niche, were made of it.

San José Mission could justly be called the *Metropoli* of all those of New Spain; not because of its antiquity, but for the beauty of its plan; strength of its construction, the grace and fairness of its edifice, and the abundance of its defenses, there being no other in all the line of presidios of the frontier, which deserved even a comparison with it; all of which added to the admirable and heroic virtues of its founder, Father Margil.

SAN FRANCISCO XAVIER DE NAJERA

While Aguayo was visiting the mission founded in his honor, he received the Yerbipiano Captain Juan Rodríguez (so called by the Spaniards) who came with 50 Ranchería Grande Indians (of Tonkawan filiation) to request a mission for themselves. This chief acted as guide for the marquis.

Upon his return to San Antonio in 1722, Aguayo, true to his word, founded the mission requested, on March 10th, calling it *San Francisco de Nájera*. It was located between the Valero and

San Jose missions, probably at the site of present Conception Mission. Possession was given to Father Joseph Gonzales, of the Queretaran College. The remaining fifty Ranchería Grande Indians immediately removed to the mission. Juan Rodríguez, their chief, appeared at the celebration of the founding, in a suit in Spanish style, of thick woolen stuff from England.

Before the founding of this mission, the records of the Huerbipiamo tribe were kept in the other missions, but quite distinct and apart from the other records. One of the first was dated in 1721. Among those baptized at the mission of *San Francisco Xavier de Nájera*, which became known as "the Huerbipiamo suburb," were also Muruames, and Ticmamares; a Guerjuatída from the Ranchería Grande also appeared. As the last records are dated during the year 1726, it is evident thàt the mission did not exist after that time.

ESPADA

Sketch of the Mission San Francisco de la Espada, by Robert J. Onderdonk.

CONCEPTION

From a photograph by Raba, of the original painting in oil, by H. Lungkwitz. Kindness of the Carnegie Library and the Witte Museum. Lungkwitz settled in Fredericksburg in 1848, but moved to San Antonio about two years later. A collection of five paintings by him, is now owned by the Carnegie Library, or San Antonio Public Library, loaned to the Witte Museum in July of 1929. This is the first of the collection. San Jose Mission is the second. The Alameda (East Commerce St.), the third, the Lewis Mill, looking toward San Fernando Cathedral, fourth and the Mission of San Juan is the fifth.

CONCEPTION, SAN JUAN, AND ESPADA

The system of colonizing by means of missions and presidios had been distrusted by some from the very beginning; but, when the military reported (1726) difficulties with the religious, in regard to attending mass, there was a positive and outspoken objection to it.

Pedro de Rivera was making his tour of inspection of the frontier presidios, and seems to have found all of them in bad condition. As a result of his recommendations, a series of reforms were inaugurated, which called for the suppression of the Presidio of Dolores, and the reduction of the garrisons of the other three presidios to nearly one half.

The missionaries, and particularly those of east Texas, were greatly disappointed, for instead of a reduction, they had expected additional forces to protect them. When the Dolores Presidio was withdrawn, in 1729, the Queretarans asked that their three missions might be removed to the protection of San Antonio de Béxar, where numbers of unconverted Indians (Pacaos, Pajalata, and Pitalaques) could easily be reached. The Zacatecans, however, resigned themselves to work on with their missions (at the Adaes, the Ais and Nacogdoches) under the reduced protection of the Presidio of Pilar de los Adaes.

As the three Queretaran missions had accomplished very little in east Texas, their just request was complied with, and they were permitted to remove to the more convenient location, where they could be of greater service to the two Majesties.

In accordance with a vice-regal commission (October 29, 1729), the governor, the ex-guardian of the Queretaran College, and the president of the Texas missions, selected three places, "two on the San Antonio river, and one on the Medina, below the junction . . . " where the missions were at first temporarily located, and where the Pacaos, Pajalats and Pitalacs agreed to settle, and submit to doctrine.

Rivera, the ex-inspector, did not approve (September 22, 1730) the location for the lower mission on the Medina, as he considered it exposed to the Apache. So the viceroy in his final decree, of October 2, 1730, in which he ordered three soldiers for each mission, for a period of two years, recommended that the Captain of the Royal Presidio use his own judgment as to the location of the lower mission.

The Captain of the Presidio of San Antonio de Béxar transmitted the viceroy's order to the Captain of the Presidio of La Bahía del Espíritu Santo, December 15, 1730, with orders to execute it, "he being delegated as judge for that purpose, in the absence of any public or royal notary."

Upon receipt of the viceroy's order, Captain Costales (of La Bahía) kissed it and placed it on his head, as a message from his king and natural lord, which with blind obedience he obeyed and was ready to execute whatever it commanded. The Captain of the Presidio of San Antonio de Béxar, being advised of this proceedure, decreed, January 12, 1731, the establishment of the missions named. The acts of each party were written down and attested by assisting witnesses. The Captain of the Presidio of San Antonio de Béxar then proceeded, March 5, 1731, to the first mission-ground (Conception), accompanied by several of his officers, and Father Bergara grasped the hand of the captain of the tribe, in the name of all the other Indians who had attached themselves to the mission, "and led him about over the locality, and caused him to pull up weeds, throw stones, and perform all the other acts of real possession, that by virtue thereof they might not be dispossessed without being first heard and defended by Father Bergara, president of the Texas missions, or such other of the clergy as might have administration over them. After declaring the bounds of the mission, there was attached to it pasturelands, watering places, irrigating privileges, uses, and services, and the further right, in planting time, to drive their stock out west for pasture, so as not to prejudice the crops. The act of possession concluded by notyfing the Indians, through an interpreter, what they should do in advancement of Christian doctrine, and in avoidance of crime."

"At the same time, Captain Pérez (of the Presidio of San Antonio de Béxar) proceeded to put other tribes in possession of the mission-grounds of San Francisco de la Espada, and San Juan, situated below, on the San Antonio river; the same formality being observed in each case. The record of the titles (. . . a simple narrative of the action of each party) was then filed in the archives of San Fernando de Béxar, and a certified copy furnished to each mission. It will be observed, in the foregoing abstract of the transfer, that the title was assumed to be in the king of Spain, and that the transfer was to the Indians, and not to the priests, who, by their vows, could own no worldly estate."

During the first ten years these three missions ministered to the Pajalates, Pachaos, Thilojas, Venados, Pachalacas, Orejones, Tracames, Sayopines, and Pamacos; and to some Pasnacanes, many of whom were from the jurisdiction of the La Bahía presidio, where it was impossible for the holy fathers to maintain missions.

Fray Benito Fernández de Santa Anna who arrived in 1731, served most of his time as president of the four Queretaran missions. "After living three years at Mission San Antonio de Valero he moved his headquarters to Conception. Scarcely less conspicuous was Father Francisco Mariano de los Dolores y Viana, who arrived in 1733 and remained until 1763, succeeding Father Santa Anna as President. His residence was at Mission San Antonio de Valero. None did more valuable service for history than diligent Father Martín García, of Mission San Antonio, who wrote a long disquisition concerning the management of Indians, and copied in his own handwriting many of the older records of the missions to preserve them from destruction. The painstaking reports and correspondence of the missionaries as a whole will always stand as a monument to their training and intellect, and though as yet little known, will constitute a priceless treasure of history and ethnology."

MISIONES

Of the Province of Texas, facsimilie of the document in the Bexar Archives. Certified Copy (August 29, 1796), of the relación of the missions, included in the informe of the viceroy, count of Revilla Gigedo to His Majesty, dated December 30, 1793, showing the names of the eight missions in Texas, the year founded, the distance from the Villa Capital (San Antonio), the Nations for whom founded, and the total number of souls. Note that the document reports 1716 as the year for the San Antonio Mission.

CONCEPTION

The mission *Nuestra Señora de la Purísima Concepción de los Ainais* (commonly called *"Asinais,"* through a miscopy of the word), was originally founded by the Queretarans of the Ramón Expedition in 1716, about nine leagues from the San Francisco Mission, east of Angelina river, for the *Ainai* (*Hinai*) nation. It was reestablished by Aguayo in 1721, with 400 Indians when new buildings were erected.

After its temporary location on the San Marcos, it was permanently reestablished, March 5, 1731, on the west bank of the San Antonio River, a little more than one league below the Villa and Presidio, and probably at the site of the extinguished Queretaran mission San Francisco Xavier de Nájera.

According to Governor Muñoz (see illustration, *Relación*, 1793) this mission was founded for the Tacanes, Sanipaos, and other Indians. No longer ministering to the Ainai, its name was changed to *Nuestra Señora de la Concepción de Acuña* (or, *"Misión de la Concepción Purísima de María,* called de *Acuña"*) in honor of the viceroy, the Marqués de Casa Fuerte, whose baptismal name was Juan de Acuña.

The Conception book of marriage records, now in the San Fernando Cathedral archives, begins July 9, 1733 and ends with the signature of Manuel Flores de Valdez, who was in charge of the mission from 1761 to March 9, 1793 (?).

The first marriage recorded was that of "Joseph Flores, of the Patumaco nation, present governor of this pueblo, and chief of the Pajalates, Siguipiles, Tilpacopales, and others." According to these records about thirty so-called tribes or nations were represented at this mission before 1790; they appeared in the following chronological order: "Pajalat, Siguipil, Tilpacopal, Patumaco, Pachalaque, Patalca, Tiloja, Xarame (1733); Pamache (Pamaque*?), Cujan (1734); Pacaba (pacoa*? 1735); Guapica (Guapite?), Pausame* (1738); Payaya (1739); Pastia (1741); Pacao,* Tacame;* Orejon* (1742); Chayopin (1745); Venado* (1746); Apache (1747); Lipan (1751); Sanipao (1755); Piguiqui,* Manos de Perro (1756); Yojuan (1758); Pajalache* (Pajalat? 1759); Malaquita (1764); Borrado,* Copane (1767); Comanche (1770); Pamaque (1775).

Those marked (*) are named in García's *Manual,* as speaking Coahuiltecan. See *San Francisco de la Espada.*

"The Apache and the Yojuane in most cases were captives, while the Pacoa and Chayopin represented neophytes of the neighboring missions who intermarried with the neophytes of Conception."

According to these records Muñoz was not correct in stating that the Sanipao were at the founding of Conception mission. In March of 1755, a band of them appeared and "in one day were instructed, baptized, and remarried to the wives 'whom they had taken in the forests.' "

From the founding (1731) to 1740, two hundred and fifty adults and children had been baptized. Of 120 inhabitants only six were catchumen, the rest having died.

By 1762, seven hundred and ninety-two adults and children had been baptized; the deaths totalled 558; the families living at the mission numbered 58; who with widows and children, totalled 207, of the Pajalate, Tacamane and Sanipao nations.

The church was described as being 32 varas long by 8 varas wide, built of lime and stone, with arches, a dome and two towers, with their bells. In the chapel was a murial painting of the five *Señores,* a gilded ciborium (*Sagrario*), and above, an altar piece in which was the image of the *Purísima Concepción* in elegant sculpturing, with the Child in her arms, and with a crown of silver. In the transept were two altars with various paintings, and two wooden images of Our Lady of Dolores and Our Lady of Pilar. There were two confessionals, benches, and a pulpit. Beneath the two towers were two chapels, one dedicated to *Señor San Miguel,* with its altar, which was very decent; and the other which served as a baptistery, where there was a baptismal font with its copper covering, three *chrismeros,* a receptacle for salt, and *concha* of silver.

The sacristy was composed of only one room, with a 12 vara vault, in which were cupboards, and chests in which were kept three chalices with their patents, a large cup, some cruets, with their silver plate, an incense burner, a censer, oil cruet and the missal; and the vestments and other ornaments for service.

There were the necessary dormitories for the missionaries, with offices, built with arches and their portales, and supplied with the necessary furnishings and ornaments, with provisions for the Indians.

There was one spacious room where they had three workshops for weaving textiles for the Indians' clothes, with the necessary tools for the working with wools and cotton. There were also the necessary yokes and implements for cultivating the soil, as well as a carpenter shop, and the supplies for iron working. The interpreters and carpenters of the mission were Indians.

The mission had ample lands and sufficient water for its fields and cattle.

The *Pueblo de Acuña* was composed of two rows of stone houses and jacals in which the Indians lived. They were conveniently furnished with household and kitchen utensils. The pueblo was surrounded by a wall for its safety and defence. It had its enclosed fields nearby, with the necessary water supply, a running ditch with its stone dam, and its rancho inhabited by the families necessary for attending to the 200 mares, 110 hogs, 610 head of cattle, and 200 head of goats and sheep which the mission possessed at the time (1762).

In the granary, a spacious room, were stored 800 *fanegas* (one *fanega* is 1:60 bushels) of corn and 50 of beans, for the maintenance of the pueblo.

Life at the *Pueblo de Acuña* was more or less typical of the life of the other missions of the time. Every morning before work, and every evening after work, all of the Indians recited in concert, the text of the Christian doctrine according to the catechism of Ripalda. Three or four times a week the Indians were instructed in reference to the same text of the catechism, in the mysteries of the holy faith, and the obligations of Christians, with similies and arguments adapted to their inexpressible rusticity. The Gentiles were taught separately by means of their interpreters, which resulted in an extra expenditure of time, until they were grounded in the elements; and when they had shown some disposition to remain at the mission, which not even the oldest Christians had in full measure, holy baptism was administered to them; and to the dying and sick, if they were infidels, the holy baptism was promptly administered. To the Christians were administered the holy sacraments of penance, the eucharist, and extreme unction. For those who came from the wilds, already married, the natural contract was ratified, leaving only one wife to those who brought several. They were then baptized. The Christians were married at the proper time by the church authorities and in conformity with the regulations of the holy Council of Trent.

Special attention was paid to the temporal assistance of the Indians, because it was the personal business of the missionaries, and because it was one of the most important means of subsistence for those who lived at the missions, and for the attraction of those who inhabited the woods, who observed and considered the advantages that the others enjoyed.

Every Sunday and on special feast days, cattle were killed and each individual was given his corresponding ration of meat; mutton was given to those who were ill. Corn was also given them; with beans, potatoes, pumpkins, watermelons, melons, peppers, salt and sugar. The latter was made from cane planted annually at each mission, because it was found the best thing to regale the Indians and the most pleasing to their appetites. Cotton and wool were used in making *mantas, terlingas, rebozos,* cloths and blankets. The surplus of these articles, was used for the purchase of manufactured articles, such as cloths, utensils, *metates,* tobacco, glass beads, tools, bridles, and saddles, needlee, and thread, etc.

Horses were used in looking after the cattle, in gathering the flocks and in other services to which they belong; most of them, however, were lost or stolen, either by enemies or by the Indians, of the missions themselves, when they escaped.

By 1780 the altars of the pretty church were decorated with an abundance of ornaments and sacred vessels, noted as being very rich, for the place.

The sacristy was a pretty room, also with vault, as all the convent, which was also prudently built with lime stone for the prevention of fire, which stone was taken from the ground only a few varas from the mission walls.

The habitations of the two ministers were confortable and spacious, though with low ceilings.

The pueblo was composed of two rows of houses, which with the church, convent and granary, formed a regular square plaza, which was entered by two well guarded gates, which were easy to defend.

The Indians of the Pueblo de Acuña also suffered great loses from epidemics, as well as from daily attacks of the enemy, who never spared them when they could take them by surprise, especially the Apache; and from the difficulties which daily increased for their replacement.

The Census Report of 1783 shows 32 men, 29 women, 18 boys and 8 girls at mission Conception. Two years later it was said that the church of this mission was the best in the province, being valued with other property at 35,000 pesos.

SAN JUAN DE CAPISTRANO

Rear view of Mission, taken from near the river—shows cross of stone that fell intact to the ground and was later destroyed. From Wright, San Antonio de Béxar, "illustrated with drawings by J. M. Longmire from Rare Photographs," p. 152. This work also includes an illustration of a "side view of Mission San Juan, before restoration."

SAN JUAN

The mission *San José de los Nazones* was originally founded by Father Espinosa, July 10, 1716, east of Angelina river, about 20 miles northwest of Nacogdoches, on a small stream flowing north, evidently one of the southern branches of Shawnee creek, for the Nazoni and Nadaco nations. It was reestablished by Aguayo (August 13, 1721), when the church and dwellings, found in ruins, were rebuilt.

Subsequent to the withdrawal of the Presidio of Dolores in 1729, this mission was suppressed along with the other two of the College of Querétaro. It had never been very successful, "for while the Indians were in the main friendly, they were indiffernt to the faith, and refused to give up their life in scattered villages to live in mission pueblos."

"An attempt was first made to reestablish it on San Marcos river, then on the Nueces and the Frio, but finally a site was chosen on the San Antonio," three league (6 mi.) below the present city of that name. Here, on March 5, 1731, the mission of San José de los Nazones, no longer ministering to the Nazones Indians, and to avoid a conflict of names, for a mission called *San José* (de San Miguel de Aguayo) was already on the San Antonio, a little more than a league to the northeast, was rechristened *San Juan Capistrano,* in honor of the great promoter of the Observant reform, Giovanni di Capistrano (1386-1465), of a family of Angevin origin in the Abruzzi (Two Sicilies, Italy), who formed a crusade against the Turks (at Belgrade), and who was canonized in 1690.

San Juan Capistrano Mission began celebrating baptisms from the day of its founding. Among the first tribes ministered to were the Tilijaes and Orejones. On May 23, 1733, the baptism of the first Pamaque (Tinapihuaya?) was celebrated. Three of the adult children of the Pamaque chief, Captain Barbas, were baptized during this year, and remained at the mission. The Pamaque were attracted by the Orejones, whose language was so much like their own, that one could not be distinguished from the other. The Pasnacanes and Piguiques were also gathered at this mission. Some Borrados Indians were also brought in from the coast, before 1754, though that tribe was being gathered at the Espada Mission.

Up to about 1740 two hundred and seventy-eight adults and children had been baptized, of whom 147 had died. At that time there were 218 inhabitants, including 66 Christians, the rest receiving instruction in the faith.

Up to 1752 the baptisms totalled 196.

The missionary report of 1762 stated that from its founding to this date (1762), there had been 847 baptisms, and 645 deaths; the total population at the time was 203, including 51 families of Orejones, Sayopines, Pamaques, and Piguiques.

The mission had lands, though not sufficient for its cattle (1,000 head), sheep (3,500), and horses (100 horses and 400 mares, in eleven herds).

In the spacious granary were 1,000 fanegas of corn and beans. The spacious workshop was well supplied with the necessary tools and implements for their fields, in which they cultivated corn, beans, peppers and cotton. There were three weaving rooms. There were also the necessary tools for the carpenters and iron workers.

The pueblo of the mission was composed of strong jacales and even some stone houses, of which more were being built, for which purpose twelve carts were in readiness. These houses were furnished with the necessary utensils. They also had twenty guns with the corresponding ammunition.

Serving as a supplementary church was one room of 25 varas, which was well constructed, with its corresponding sacristy, and three altars; one to *San Juan Capistrano*, with its gilded *sagrario*, another to Jesús de Nazareth, and the third, to Our Lady of Rosario, all with images of special sculpturing. The altars were decorated with various devout paintings. There was a baptismal font, with its *concha*, of silver, two oil cruets, 22 candelabra, two incense burners, with their censers, six little bells, and a high cross, all of copper; three *crismeros*, two chalices, with patens, a large cup, three missals and three manuals, and the other necessary possessions for service, including 21 ornaments, and 11 frontpieces.

The convent of this mission was formed with the church sacristy, and four cells, with their córredor, two offices, a refectory, kitchen, workshop and *portería*. These rooms were decorated and supplied with the necessities of life for the missionaries and the Indians.

Morfi observed (January 14, 1778) that the spacious, clean and decorated church, was constructed in a manner different from the churches of the Conception and San José missions (built into, and forming a part of the boundary or rampart wall). The little convent was then composed of four cells, two for the ministers and the other two for the guests, a corredor, two offices, refectory, kitchen and work shop, or weaving room.

The population of this mission had considerably diminished, owing to warfare and epidemics. The Census of 1783 shows 53 men, 26 women, 13 boys and 7 girls. A report of December 31, 1792, shows this mission "dependent of the Villa of San Fernando," with 16 Indian families, and Spaniards, including some Tlascalte-cans. A report in the Nacogdoches Archives of the following year, shows a total of 49 inhabitants, 27 of whom were Indians.

Near this mission, an extremely picturesque aqueduct, of low, massive arches, was built, to carry the waters over Piedra Creek to irrigate the lands of the Espada Mission and the ranches beyond.

ESPADA

The history of this mission dates back to the very beginning of Texas. It was founded by General Alonso de León, and Father Manzanet (of the Queretaran College), May 23, 1690, a short distance west of Neches river, in the very populous and principal valley of the nation of the Tejas, among the Nabedache tribe, whose village became known as *San Pedro*, (about two miles northwest of Weches, Houston county).

Subsequent to the abandonment of 1693, it was reestablished by Captain Ramón (July 5, 1716), with the name *Nuestro Padre San Francisco de los Téjas*, a few leagues farther inland, across the Neche river (southwest of Alto, Cherokee county, near the Neche mounds), among the Neche and Nacachau tribes. Possession was given to Father Espinosa, the Queretaran President of the Expedition, and he appointed Father Hidalgo, "who for so many years solicited this conversion," to serve the Nabedache, Neche, Nacachau, and Nacono tribes.

"On August 5, 1721, it was reestablished by Aguayo and Espinosa, and put in charge of Fray José Guerra. On this day Aguayo gave the Neche chief the *bastón,* the symbol of authority conferred by the Spaniards, and clothed 180 Indians of all ages. Espinosa exhorted them to gather into a pueblo, to be named *San Francisco Valero.* (The mission was rechristened San Francisco de los Neches). This they promised to do as soon as they harvested their corn. Still the mission failed to succeed. In 1727 Rivera found it without Indians, and described the settlement as one of huts." So with the withdrawal of the Dolores Presidio on the Angelina (1729), it was removed (1730) with the other Queretaran missions (San José de los Nazones and Nuestra Señora de la Purísima Concepción). "After an attempt had been made to find a site on the San Marcos, Nueces, and Frio rivers, the mission was reestablished in 1731, on San Antonio river as *San Francisco de la Espada,*" a little less than half league to the south of the San Juan Capistrano Mission, and three leagues from the Presidio of San Antonio de Béjar.

"Tradition has it that in building the walls the mortar was mixed with asses' milk which the priests consecrated to the service. It was dedicated to St. Francis of Assissi, the founder of the great order of Franciscans, and tradition says that the old tower was built in the form of the hilt of a sword, the imagination of the founders supplying length to the blade, thus completing the similarity to the whole weapon, and the mission named San Francisco de la Espada—St. Francis of the Sword."

"There were brought from the Frio and Nueces rivers to this and the neighbor missions three docile native tribes, unused to agriculture, the Pacao, Pajalat, and Pitalac, which together were said to number about 1,000 persons. This mission was founded with the Pacao tribe, its chief being made 'governor' of the pueblo called Pueblo de Acuña."

"In June, 1737, there were 137 neophytes, mainly Pacaos and Atchahomos (apparently those better known as Tacames), 80 of them having been baptized. These two tribes seem to have been the chief ones there. On June 7th, of that year, all deserted, the missionaries charging the flight to fear of the Apache, while the Indians and soldiers said the cause was bad treatment. By November 22nd, only seven had returned, in spite of the fact that three efforts had been made to reclaim them. In January a fourth embassy sent for them brought back 108 more. In June, 1738, the mission still had a Pacao 'governor.' This year the Apache made a raid on the neophytes while they were gathering fruit in the neighborhood, near the Medina, killed a number and took others captive. By February 20, 1740, there had been 233 baptisms . . . and at that time which was immediately after the epidemic, there were 120 neophytes remaining," 27 of whom were Christians, and 23 Gentiles.

The report of 1762 states that from the founding of the mission to this date (March 6, 1762), 815 had been baptized; 513 had died, and at the time there were only 52 families, who with widows and single people and children, totalled some 207, of the nations of the Pacaos, Borrados, and Maraquites, the last two tribes still supplying the mission.

Though the church of this mission had been commenced, it had not been finished because of the lack of stone of good quality which had only been discovered a short time before. It was their intention to complete it. In the meanwhile they were using a suitable room, which was spacious and decent, where with its choir, was an altar to Our Holy Father Francisco, with a carved and gilded *sagrario,* and various carved and painted images, which were very beautiful and decent. There was also another altar to Our Lady of Rosario. There was a baptismal font, a cross, two candle holders, confessionals and benches. The chest of the mission contained the customary utensils and ornaments for divine service.

The convent was composed of four cells, in the second story, with three on the ground floor, with their corredors, a workshop and a spacious granary, all of stone. In the cells were the necessary utensils and furnishings. There were also offices and the other customary accomodations.

In the granary were more than 1,000 fanegas of corn, 60 fanegas of beans; and cotton, wool, peppers, and salt for the Indians. There were three weaving rooms in the workshop, with the necessary tools and implements, along with the necessities for cultivating the soil. They had as well, 16 guns and their corresponding ammunition.

The pueblo had three rows of stone houses, properly furnished.

The ranch of the mission was improved with one stone house where the attending families lived. There were at the time, 1262 head of cattle, 400 goats and sheep, 145 horses in eleven herds, and nine burros.

Owing to the multiplicity of tribes at the San Antonio missions, and their variety of languages, the place seemed another Babylon. It was not possible to prepare a *Manual* for each nation, nor was it an easy or practicable matter to translate the Catechism into each of the respective languages. So Father Bartolomé García of the Espada Mission, solved the problem, by preparing a *Manual* in the principal and most common language of the group. This *Manual* which preserves for us the Coahuiltecan language, was printed in Mexico, October 15, 1760. It was written for the administration of the Pajalates, Orejones, Pacaos, Pacoás, Tilijayas, Alafapas, Pausanes and other very different ones, in the Queretaran missions on the San Antonio and Rio Grande, the Pacuaches, Mescales, Pampopas, Tacames, Chayopines, Venados, Pamaques, and all the youth of the Pihuiques, Borrados, Sanipaos, and Manos de Perro.

Morfi observed, during his visit to San Antonio in January of 1778, that this mission (Nuestro Señor *Padre San Francisco de la Espada*) was the first mission which one encountered when travelling from Coahuila to the province of Texas, and for this reason,, it was the nearest to Medina River. Its pasture lands extended for more than two leagues beyond this river, which was itself another two leagues distant from the mission; and on these lands they had innumerable (4,000 head of) cattle and sheep. But from the time that the Apaches frequented there, they slaughtered these animals with horrible destruction. In 1777 they killed 700 head belonging to San José alone, and as far as that was concerned, the robberies at the Espada Mission were not of less consequence.

The church had been torn down, as it had already threatened to fall in ruins; but in the meanwhile, as another was being constructed, they celebrated divine service in a very spacious gallery, devoutly decorated, with a comfortable sacristy and choir. The convent was formed with four upper cells, and two lower ones, with corredors, all on the same line. To the side of the convent was the workshop and without beauty. The pueblo, with the three rows of houses, formed with the convent, a plaza, a part of the outer wall, also of stone, closing the square.

Morfi reported (1778) a population of 40 families, totalling 133 souls of all ages and of both sexes. The 1783 Census shows 32 men, 28 women, 30 boys, and 6 girls. The 1793 report for the previous year (1792), shows a total of only 34 souls. The Bexar Archives report of 1792 shows a total of 97 inhabitants, including 32 Spaniards, 38 Indians, 7 mulatos, of whom 22 were farmers, two builders, one artesan, two day laborers and one religious.

"On April 10, 1794, the commandant general of the Provincias Internas, Pedro de Nava, ordered this and the neighbor missions secularized, and the order was in part carried out in June and July by Governor Manuel Muñoz. On July 11th, the movables and lands were distributed among the Indians, each of the 15 adult males being given about 10 acres as private property, and about 100 acres being assigned to the Indians in common. It seems, however, that the Zacatecan friars (who took over the Queretaran missions in Texas in 1773), continued their ministry there well into the 19th century. In 1804 there were 39 persons living at the pueblo, and 107 at the mission of San Francisco de la Espada."

The process of secuarization went on very slowly in Texas. In spite of the Spanish Cortes' decree of 1813, it was not until 1823 that the last mission at San Antonio became extinct. Refugio Mission (founded for the Karankawan tribes in 1791) continued to exist until 1827. When the populations required it, diocesan priests took the places of the Franciscan friars.

Perfil

De esta manera y con esta fachada quedarà
la poblacion que se manifiesta en el pla
no que esta escripto abajo, cuyas letras
y numeros corresponden segun el lugar
donde estan, Colocados. Respondien=
dose el vno, àl otro

Fabricado.

SAN FERNANDO DE BEXAR
Original Plan

SETTLEMENT

R AMON, after his Expedition of 1716, was not long in convincing the authorities of New Spain that to make permanent the missions established among the Texas Indians, it would be necessary not only to extend the sphere of occupation, but to make a greater show of strength. The early occupation of Espíritu Santo Bay was encouraged. La Bahía was recognized as a very advantageous base of supplies coming by water from Veracruz. San Antonio, on the other hand, the halfway haven between La Bahía and the Province of the Texas, would also serve as a useful point of observation for the activities of the French. So Father Olivares' mission on the San Antonio, as well as a well fortified presidio to be maintained at the site, were approved by a Junta of War on December 2, 1716.

Don Martín de Alarcón was appointed governor, and instructed to select a capital for the province, where there should be erected strong houses of stone for the soldiers' quarters, and to establish a *villa* or city on the banks of the San Antonio river, in the proximity of the mission, which in accordance with the Laws of the Indies, was to consist of not less than thirty Spanish civilian inhabitants to distinguish it from a mere Indian *pueblo*. In consequence *San Antonio de los Llanos* was founded during the early part of 1718, which comprised the old *San Antonio de Padua* mission, now called *San Antonio de Valero,* the presidio of *San Antonio de Béxar* and the *Villa de Béjar*. This was the first attempt at founding a municipality. Alarcón was unable to bring the necessary thirty inhabitants "owing to the fact that the Rio del Norte (Rio Grande) had risen and thus prevented all of the expedition from crossing, particularly the women." The *Villa de Bejar* was populated with only ten families, and it is not likely that this aggregation of early settlers had any municipal government of their own; they were apparently not recognized as a legal *villa* or city.

The chivalrous activities of the Marquis of Aguayo should now be recalled. His expedition (1719-1722), which drove the French from Texas, and the last of its kind east of the Rio Grande, by increasing the military strength of the province, and by the settlement of families, secured to Spain her hold on Texas. The Marquis repeteadly emphasized the importance of Spanish families and their domestic establishments for the maintenance of the province. He recommended to the King of Spain, a curtailment of military expenditures, and "as indispensable, populating the province of Texas with two hundred Spanish families from Galicia, the Canary Islands or Havana, as such settlers would be more given to work than the natives of Texas, as well as with an additional two hundred settlers from Gran Tlaxcala, who could be brought by way of Veracruz to La Bahía at little cost and who had proved themselves very satisfactory wherever they had settled, as they were religious they would set an excellent example for the natives."

These recommendations were duly acted upon. Pedro de Rivera was instructed to inspect the frontier presidios and as a result of his *revista,* and subsequent reports, a series of military reforms were inaugurated, mainly in the direction of retrenchment.

While the vagabond Indians of west and central Texas were submissive and cowardly, the Natchez and their kindred tribes, on the contrary, enlisted the Apaches and the Commanches (1729) in an attempt to annihilate both the French and Spanish "intruders." Again, St. Denis saved the situation, and the Spaniards as well. The missionary fathers, as was to be expected, became alarmed, left entirely exposed as they were at their weakest, to such a formidable league; their vehement protests against military retrenchment soon precipitated a political conflict which terminated in a change of governors.

In Spain the king had decided that the four hundred families recommended by Aguayo "should come as volunteers from the Canary Islands, owing to the facilities of transportation from that point." Royal Cedulas were issued to help them on their way. The Canary Islands had long been a reliable source of colonial supplies. As early as 1536 Canary Islanders had been settled on the La Plata, at the founding of San Gabriel. The first families of Montevideo too, had been augmented by twenty families from the Canary Islands. Relations between the Islands and Florida were authorized in 1580, and during the 17th century contracts were entered into for settling Florida with Canary Islanders and Campeche Indians. One hundred Canary Island families actually landed in Santo Domingo.

A decree issued in 1729, regulating the transportation of the proposed four hundred families, provided that not less than ten families should sail in any one vessel to Havana and then to Veracruz, from where they were to proceed through Mexico to the Province of Texas. It was only with great difficulty that the minimum requirements were complied with; even then a group of single men had to be considered as a family to complete the ten.

The original party of fifty-two persons were conducted from Veracruz to Quautitlán where the first list was made, September 9, 1730. "An allowance for provisions of four reales per diem per family began on September 6th. In Saltillo a new list and inventory was certified to, January 31, 1731, and Colonel Aguirre provided them an escort of ten soldiers to the Presidio del Norte (Rio Grande). From there they were escorted anew to San Antonio, where they arrived at eleven o'clock, March 9th, 1731."

In San Antonio the Governor made a new and final list "in order to confer upon them as first settlers, and upon their descendants, the tilte of *Hijos Dalgos* or *Hidalgos*, the regular honor bestowed upon first settlers of a new city in the colonies." (Laws of the Indies, Law VI, Title vi, Book iv).

At this time too, there were changes in the missionary field. The attempt to civilize the Indians of the Hasinai settlements into *pueblos*, built in close order was recognized as a dismal failure. The Indians determined to live in *ranchos* (separate houses) well apart from each other, each household seeking a place suitable for its crops and having a supply of water. It was also soon learned that "the less and smaller tribes of the San Antonio river nearer Mexico and farther removed for the contrary influence of the French, afforded a better field for missionary labors." So in conformity with the Spanish Government's decision to concentrate forces at San Antonio, the missions in east Texas were abandoned (1729). The original missions, *San Francisco de los Téjas, Concepción* and *San José de los Nazones,* were reestablished on the San Antonio river (March 5, 1731) when they were respectively renamed *San Francisco de la Espada, La Purisima Concepción* and *San Juan Capistrano.*

"The colonists continued to receive for one year after their arrival, the four reales per diem, with provisions at the same price as furnished the soldiers." Each family was given a yoke of oxen and the necessary implements for cultivating the soil. They were furnished seed, the planting of which was supervised at the proper seasons. They were also alloted metates for grinding corn.

A site near the San Pedro Springs (near the old ford according to tradition) was chosen for the colonists. Here they first pitched their tents on San Antonio ground. But no sooner had the new arrivals sought repose in their temporary encampment, than the Apaches and their allies swooped down upon the settlements, stealing the cattle and committing many atrocious crimes. It was only after a formal expedition had defeated and chastised the perfidious enemy that the final settlement of the colonists was continued.

Their municipality it was decided, should be "to the east of the Presidio, nearer the bend in the river, as protection from the savages." The contour reproduced in this booklet shows the proposed *Villa,* as planned by the appropriate authorities (1730), previous to the arrival of the Island colonists at San Antonio. The instructions accompanying the map were wise indeed, and reflected good judgment and taste. Complying with such details, however, was quite another matter.

To begin with, it was the season for ploughing, and planting of corn; so the families were extended temporary comfort in the houses of the soldiers and inhabitants of the Presidio. By March 15th, 1731 lands between the river and creek north and south of the Presidio, had been quickly allotted for immediate sowing. By the 30th of June, "there were two fanegas of corn sown; some beans, barley, cotton, chiles, peppers, melons, water-melons, and squash. Also many vegetables. Despite the distance from Saltillo, slips which had been brought had taken root and were showing fruit."

"By July 2nd, the municipality had been laid off. On the northwest of the Plaza two squares were pointed out, one for the Deputation or Customs and the other for a dwelling for one of the principal families. On the other and corresponding side, southeast, another two squares were pointed out for the site of other important families."

"As this was the first political settlement of Texas, it was given the title of city, and it was to be the capital of the province, the privilege however, of confirming this decree, and giving the illustrious municipality a coat of arms, should that be his royal pleasure, was reserved by the viceroy to His Majesty." The *Villa* was given the name of *"San Fernando,"* in honor of Don Fernando, Prince of the Asturias, who later became King of Spain, the viceroy, Juan de Acuña, Marquis of Casa Fuerte, having refused to give his own name to the municipality, preferring to call it San Fernando in honor of His Serene Highness.

The first formal census of San Antonio, dated December 31, 1788, (see the *Early Texas Album*), refers to the municipality as the "Villa of San Fernando, Capital of the Provinces of Texas." An oficial document regarding military activities, dated in 1788, refers to the entire group of settlements on the San Antonio River, including the mission and its pueblo, the presidio and the villa, as *"San Antonio de Béxar."* Then, the Convocatoria of 1823, calling for a Congressional Election in Mexico, provided for the subdivision of Texas into five sections, with *"San Antonio de Bexar"* as the capital of the entire province (of Texas).

The Constitution of 1836, which reorganized the old precincts or municipalities into counties, made *San Antonio de Bexar,* or simply *"Bexar"* the county seat of Bexar County (created March 17, 1836); and this name for our city was confirmed by the town charter granted by the Republic of Texas, June 5, 1837, at which time John W. Smith was elected mayor. By an act of December 14, 1837, the citizens of *Bexar*, or the settlements of the old San Antonio de Valero, in the county of Bexar, were declared a body politic and corporate, with the name and title of "the City of San Antonio," Subsequent charters for the City of San Antonio were approved in 1842, 1852, 1856, 1870 and 1903.

LANDMARKS

SAN FERNANDO

THE zealous work of the missionaries in conjunction with the Spaniards' method of extending their jurisdiction by the use of the mission and presidio has already been described. A new class of working clergy was now to enter the field. The curate or parish priest was to assume his important duties in the Spanish settlement of San Fernando.

One of the first precautions of the Marquis of Casa Fuerte, when issuing the decree for the founding of the villa capital of San Fernando, was an order that the colonists attend mass in the chapel of the Presidio of San Antonio, until they should have erected their own parish church, for which an appropriation from the Royal Treasury was made.

The first foundation stone for the holy temple was not laid until three years after the arrival of the colonists, May 13, 1734. As the Royal appropriation had not been received, there were no resources for the construction of the church edifice, so "donations were asked of all pious souls of both San Fernando and the Presidio." By February, 25, 1738, the trustees, Vicente Alvarez Travieso and Francisco José de Arocha were able to report to the Town Council and the Justice, that an estimated total of 642.25 pesos had been received. Governor Orobio y Bazterra headed the list with a two hundred pesos contribution; the Curate, Don Recio de León followed with 25 pesos; then Captain José de Urrutia with 100. Along with the Canary Island families, the Collector of Revenues, Antonio Rodríguez Maderos, Antonio Ximenez and Francisco Decal y Músquiz, inhabitants of the villa, made contributions; while Juan Flores, Antonio Martín Saucedo, Toribio de Urrutia, José Antonio Flores, Ignacio Urrutia, Manuel and Nicolás de Carvajal, and Xavier Pérez, all of the Presidio, were generous in their donations. Six subsequent donations increased the grand total to 666.25 pesos. "This sum however, proved insufficient for the project; after many requests and special visits to the Mexican Court, the Viceroy finally contributed the 5,000 pesos from the Royal Treasury."

The parish church was erected under the invocation of the Virgin of the Candelaria and Our Lady of Guadalupe for whom the inhabitants had a particular reverence, and in accordance with the plans of the viceroy. The location of the legal center of the Villa, as shown on the Map of 1730, was at the original site of the property reserved for the church and missionaries at the founding of the Presidio, on the east side of Military Plaza, "the principal door of the church opening to the east and pointing on the Plaza of this Villa, and its rear door, to the west and fronting on the Plaza of the Presidio."

SAN FERNANDO CHURCH

In 1746 the citizens of San Fernando and all the residents of the jurisdiction were ordered to assist in the work of finishing the church. Two years later (1748) an additional 12,000 pesos were received from the viceroy. "It was not until November 6, 1749, however, that the blessing of our church of San Fernando, as well as that of the cemetery took place. It was named in honor of Saint Ferdinand," ancestor of Don Fernando, for whom the Villa had been named.

In 1828 San Fernando Church was seriously damaged by fire; it was not until 1841 that the entire building was completely repaired. The foundation stone of the present edifice was laid September 27, 1868. Five years later the original main dome fell in, and for a short time the church was in disuse. It was reopened October 6, 1873.

San Antonio was made a diocese, September 3, 1874, and Anthony Dominic Pelicer was installed as first bishop Christmas Eve, of this year (1874).

The original cemetery, surrounding the church, was removed to the site of present Milam Square and Santa Rosa Hospital. The first burial in the old *Campo Santo* was of the body of Don Angel Navarro, November 1, 1808. The tomb of the widow of Governor Antonio Cordero is in the church itself.

FOR a period of eleven years it was necessary to deposit the official documents of the Villa at the home of the Captain of the Presidio, while the meetings of the *Cabildo* or Town Council were held in private residences, owing to the absence of any municipal headquarters or Council Hall. It was not until 1742 that the inhabitants of San Fernando came to the building of the *Casas Reales*. A contract entered into with Antonio Rodríguez y Medero for the hauling of the necessary stone was not fulfilled; so a second similar contract was arranged with Manuel de Carvajal, which began the construction of the much needed Council Hall. Four years later (1749) the municipality was obliged to borrow funds for the roofing and white-washing of the structure.

By 1779, thirty years later, the *Casas Reales* were "in such a deplorable condition that it was necessary to issue a decree for their reconstruction." The Governor approved the accounts, amounting to 280 pesos and seven reales, flattering the respective contributors, and complimented the Noble Cabildo of the Villa for maintaining the Royal Houses in that state of decency and magnificence which was befitting, adding that though much was lacking to reach the state of perfection required, much had been done in spite of recent occurences, to rebuild them on a scale never before seen and which would have been impossible without the efficient support and economic management of the first alcalde, Don Joseph Antonio Curbelo.

CASAS REALES

In 1783, a resolution was passed to build a new meeting hall, as the old one in the *Casas Reales* had been destroyed. By 1791 the *Sala Capitular* was again in good condition. Many of the inhabitants refused to accept compensation for their work and materials, as they consider this "a work of public benefit." Those however, who expected pay, encountered great difficulty in collecting the funds due them. The *Ramón Junta* which was held in the Ramón residence, without the consent of the officials, and which had all the ear-marks of a revolutionary movement, was a direct result of these pay-roll irregularities.

UP to 1783 "both men and women had to be imprisoned in the *Cuerpo de Guardia* of the Presidio," but during that year "the Cabildo requested that a *Cárcel* (prison) be built on the land remaining for the *Casas Reales*, which would be competent for the separate imprisonment of male and female prisoners."

The Governor immediately approved the request, and by 1791 the said *Cárcel* "was 'enjoyed' by those who were so in need of it." It was located south of the *Casas Reales* adjoining the patio or corral, and faced south on the street, which was then called Cárcel Street, now Market Street.

At this site the "Break of '40" or the "Court House Fight" took place, Tuesday, Saint Joseph's Day, March 19, 1840, when a band of Comanches came into the settlements, for the third time, pretending to make a treaty of peace and "trying to get ransom money for their American and Mexican captives." As the Indians had not complied with previous contracts, the American Officers proposed to hold four or five of their chiefs, until the promised captives had been brought in. The Comanches on hearing this interpreted, raised a precipitant and terrific war-whoop, drawing their arrows and firing with deadly effect, "at the same time making efforts to break out of the council hall." The Americans in consequence, fired upon the Indians, when all rushed out into the public square, the citizens and soldiers pursuing the Indians in all directions. An interesting story is told of how one brave was burned out of a nearby house where he had sought refuge and locked himself in.

This site was where the first market house was located (1840), in the back yard of the old Court House, when Cárcel Street was called "Market Street." The building in style of a Greek temple was designed by John Fries and David Russi, and built in 1858, by John Campbell. Parts of it now adorn the entrance to the Little Theatre in San Pedro Park, where, curious to observe, the first market place or Indian trading post was held.

In accordance with the Law of Incorporation of 1837, the City Council appropriated and sold lots for the purpose of providing a new court house and jail. These were begun in September of 1850, at the northwest corner of Military Plaza, when the old *cuartel* or military quarters were remodelled and added to. This court house became the roosting place for bats and was commonly known as the "Old Bat Cave." It was removed when the present City Hall was nearing completion in about 1890. A third court house designed by Alfred Giles, was constructed in 1882, on the east side of Soledad Street, between Commerce and Houston Streets. The site of a fourth, and the present court house was acquired from the Dwyer-Leal heirs, the first annex to the south being acquired from the Bennet heirs while J. R. Davis was Judge.

THE southeast corner of Main Plaza and Commerce Street, just north of the site of the *Cassas Reales,* was granted in 1731, to María Robaina de Bethencourt, the widow of Juan Rodriguez Granado, as head of a family. The Granado-Bethencourt home was one' of the most distinguished in the province. Built in typical style, with patio and corridors, it was furnished with exquisite heirlooms brought from the Canary Islands, where the Bethencourt boasted descent from the sovereign family. Five paintings were particularly conspicuous there, along with a writing desk inlaid with ivory, a chest decorated with tortoise shell and silver, another of Córdova leather, with screens, and rugs and cushions to match. The dining room was beautifully equipped with ancient silver, and numerous pieces of china and crystal decorated with gold. The hostess herself was slender and charming, with fair complexion and contrasting brilliant black hair. Her jewels too, were the envy of the neighbors; and even in those early days she had with her, an ivory fan, and cigaret case of burnished gold.

The oldest son, Pedro Granado, occupied the homestead after the death of his mother. Then second Lieutenant Joseph Granado remained there for forty-eight consecutive years, bequeathing the property to his son, José Laureano Granado, who in turn, with his mother, sold the homestead to Ramón Múzquiz in 1839. During the subsequent period of revolutionary activities and political upheavals, this very desirable corner changed hands quite frequently. It was a grant to Deaf Smith's widow.

Commerce Street, in Colonial Days, was merely a road leading to the ford, to cross to the Valero Mission. The whole peninsular or loop of the river was, including our Commerce and Market Streets, used for the safe pasturing of the animals and was thus called the *Potrero*. Many of the first settlers soon established their homes in this desirable locality.

THE first grant recorded to Juan Curbelo, in 1736, was on Soledad Street, so-called in the document. One of the oldest private homes in the community, that of the De La Garza, at the site of the present southwest corner of Houston and Soledad Streets, being the only one in the vicinity, gave name to the street, *soledad,* meaning solitude or loneness.

THE original grants on the north side of the Plaza of the Islanders, as Main Plaza was also called, were to the Alvarez Travieso, De Niz and Arocha families. The Travieso and Arocha homes, of stone, were particularly attractive for the time. Their furnishings too, were in tatste and ancient period. The Alvarez Travieso house was destroyed by the flood in 1819. That of Simón de Arocha, at the corner of present Main Avenue, was acquired by the Yturri, a good family from Old Spain, and it is said that Santa Anna made his headquarters here when he attacked the Alamo.

THE San Pedro Ditch, commenced in 1738, to furnish water for San Fernando, issuing from the east side of the head waters of the San Pedro Creek, flowed down North Flores Street, and then across, to the plaza, in front of the church. It thus gave name to *Asequia Madre* Street, our present Main Avenue.

The lands south of the church property, facing east on the Main Plaza, were originally granted to Antonio de los Santos and the three Cabrera orphans. In 1747 the latter transferred their interests to Joseph Pérez. His descendants remained in the old homestead until recent times, when the house was destroyed by fire; it was rebuilt by Fries and Kampmann in 1852, for José Cassiano and his son, Ignacio. It was in this old home, known as the Cassiano Home, that the Mavericks first resided, when arriving in San Antonio in 1838. This property was acquired in 1867 by August Fretelliere and Theodore Gentilz, who in time sold their interests to James P. Hickman. The "Southern Hotel" was a well known center of hospitality in our old city.

JUST south of the site reserved for the public school, opposite the parish church, was the house and lot of Pedro Fuentes, the priest, whose lands extended along the west side of Flores Street, opposite the old Pérez home. In 1780 Father Fuentes decided to build a two-story stone house, to be the first of its kind in the community; it was to face east on the Plaza of the Villa. Being foresighted and wise, the good father sought the permission of all the appropriate authorities and interested parties before going ahead with the construction of the second story of his home, such a novel project for the place. He called attention to the fact that all the cities in the world recognized the infinite advantages of such structures, of more than a mere ground floor. Aside from spiritual considerations, a two-story house, he said, would improve the appearance of the Villa, and his particular house would set an example to the other inhabitants to construct similar houses for themselves, all of which would enhance the value of property, and give greater accomodations for families. He called attention to the fact that such buildings, though larger, would not take up any more ground; they would be more healthy, exposed as they were to more fresh air, and better suited for both summer and winter. They would also serve as a better defense for the community, affording protection not only to the inmates, but a high place from which to harry an invading enemy, and being useful as well, as towers of observation, so to spare the Holy Temple that inconvenience.

The Governor and Cabildo were prompt in approving the request, as were the adjoining landlords and other interested inhabitants. The final official approval of our first two-story house is dated October 21, 1780.

THE south side of the Main Plaza was granted to the several members of the Leal family; the Dwyers, descendants, resided there until very recent date, as has been noted in connection with the building of the present court house.

The street to the east, was originally called *"Calle de los Curbelos"* as Joseph Curbelo received a grant there (to the east) in 1761. The old Curbelo home, known as the *"quinta"* in revolutionary times, when imprisoned women and children were forced to make tortillas for the troops, was acquired by Ralph W. Bowen in 1847; and in this house he had the first American post office. The street took the name *"Quinta"* as did the entire section of the city for a while. Then the Dwyers gave it their name.

THE lot facing west on the Plaza, to the south of the *Casas Reales*, with the street between, was originally granted to Joseph Padrón and his wife, as first settlers. They sold in 1745 to Antonio Ximenez, one of the inhabitants of the villa. Then Joseph Padrón and his wife Antonio de Armas acquired the property. In 1819 Francisco Xavier Chávez the Indian expert, who married Juana Padrón, was granted the lot, on which he had already established their home.

SAINT FERDINAND
Sketch from statue in the San Fernando Cathedral
by Miss Onderdonk

1. **LEAL** — Juan Leal Goraz, b. Lancerote, 1676 son of Antonio and María Pérez. Married 1st, Lucía (Catarina) Hernández, b. Lancerote, 1685, daughter of Bartolomé and Catalina Rodríguez. Married 2nd, in San Fernando, María Melián, widow of Lucas Delgado.

2. **CURBELO** — Juan Curbelo, b. Lancerote, 1680 son of Domingo and María Martín Enrique. Married Gracia Prudhomme y Umpierre, b. Lancerote, 1684, daughter of Marcos and María Cabrera.

3. **LEAL, JR.** — Juan Leal, *el mozo*, Jr., b. Lancerote, 1700, son of Juan, above, and his 1st wife. Married María Gracia, b. Teneriffe, 1700, daughter of Pedro Gonzales Cabezas and Francisca de Acosta.

4. **SANTOS** — Antonio de los Santos, b. Lancerote, 1680 son of Simón and Anna Rodríguez. Married Isabel Rodriguez, b. Lancerote, 1686, daughter of Domingo de Bega and Leonor Rodríguez. (Note that children frequently used the mother's family name).

5. **PADRON** — Joseph Padrón, b. Palma, about 1708, married María Francisca Sanabria, b. Lancerote, 1710, daughter of Luis and Francisca Lagarda.

6. **NIZ** — Manuel de Niz, b. Grand Canary, about 1680, son of Juan and Andrea Mireles. Married Sebastián de la Peña de León, b. 1686, daughter of Domingo and Gregorio Suárez de la Peña.

7. **ALVAREZ TRAVIESO** — Vicente Alvarez Travieso, b. Teneriffe, 1706, son of Juan and Catarina Cayetano. Married María Ana Curbelo, b. 1712, daughter of Juan and Gracia. Joined the others after their arrival in Mexico.

8. **RODRIGUEZ** — Salvador Rodríguez, b. Teneriffe, 1688, son of Francisco and Isabel de los Reyes. Married María Pérez Cabrera, b. Lancerote, about 1688, daughter of Domingo and María Pérez.

9. **AROCHA** — Francisco de Arocha, b. Palma, 1703, son of Simón and Angela Francisca. Married Juana Curbelo, b. Lancerote, 1716, daughter of Juan and Gracia. Joined the others after their arrival in Mexico.

10. **RODRIGUEZ** — Antonio Rodríguez, b. City of Canaries, 1712, son of Juan and María de el Carmen. One of the original five single men who were considered in

a group as a family. Married Josefa de Niz, only child of Manuel and Sebastiana.

11. **LEAL** Joseph Leal, b. Lancerote, 1708, second son of Juan and Lucía Hernández. Married Anna de los Santos, after the departure from Cuautitlán, b. Lancerote, 1715, daughter of Antonio and Isabel.

12. **DELGADO** Juan Delgado, b. Lancerote, 1711, son of Lucas and Marian Meilán. Married Catarina Leal, after their departure from Cuautitlán, b. Lancerote, about 1714, daughter of Juan and Catarina Rodríguez.

13. **CABRERA** José Cabrera, b. Lancerote, 1715, son of Juan and María Rodríguez. With his brother Marcos and sister Ana, the head of a family. Their father died on the Veracruz road; their mother, the widow died en route, after their departure from Cuautitlán.

14. **GRANADO** María Robaina de Bethencourt, widow of Juan Rodríguez Granado, who died in Veracruz.

15. **DELGADO** Mariana Melián, widow of Lucas Delgado, who died at Veracruz, b. Lancerote, about 1700, daughter of Francisco and Inés de Hoyos.

16. **Group: the two Armas and the two Pérez** Ignacio and Martín Lorenzo de Armas, b. Canary Islands, 1706 and 1710, resp. sons of Roque and Teresa de Avilés. Ignacio married Ana Cabrera, daughter of Juan and María Rodríguez. Martín married the widow, María Robaina de Bethencourt Rodríguez Granado.
Phelipe and Joseph Antonio Pérez (Casanova), sons of Domingo and María Granado. Apparently Phelipe did not marry. Joseph Antonio married 1st, Paula Granado, daughter of Juan and María Robaina de Bethencourt, and 2nd, Gertrudis de la Zerda.

JUAN LEAL GORAZ was appointed head of the colonists by a colonial judge previous to the departure from the Canary Islands. He was reappointed by the Viceroy in Mexico. As he was the oldest man among the colonists, he was chosen by them, as their Senior Alderman, for life.

A grandson of Juan, *El Mozo*, married María Luisa de Urrutia, and their granddaughter Francisca, married José Olivarrí (brother of Plácido, the ancestor of the present Olivarrí); their daughter Paula married Anton Frederick Wulff.

Many descendants of Pedro, son of Juan, *El Mozo*, who was born during the voyage, at Havana, flourished in San Antonio to the end of the 18th century.

Joseph Leal, the second son of Juan Leal Goraz, was the great-grandfather of Remigio, the father of Juan Agustín, ancestor of the present Leal in San Antonio, including the descendants of the García Villarreal; and Mariana Leal, who married first a Ramón and second a Dwyer.

J UAN CURBELO and his wife Gracia Prudhomme y Umpierre had five children. The oldest, Joseph, born in Lancerote in 1705, married Rafaela de la Garza. Mariana married Vicente Alvarez Travieso. Juana married Francisco de Arocha. María born in Lancerote in 1717, married first, Joseph Bueno de Rojas; and second, Christobal de los Santos Coy, the pioneer schoolmaster. She was the last survivor of the original Canary Island settlers, and was popularly known as *"Tia Canaria."*

Lieutenant Joseph Antonio Rafael Curbelo, (born in 1746, and killed by the Lipans in about 1789) was the son of Joseph and Rafaela. He married in 1766, Rita Flores. Their third child, Juan Joseph Vicente, born in 1771, married Teresa, the daughter of Vicente Amador and Manuela Banul, and their son José Antonio Saturnino, born in 1791, married Josefa Delgado in 1811. Their daughter María de Jesús, born in 1813, married John W. Smith.

T HE SANTOS family from the Canary Islands and the De Los Santos Coy, of the early military families, are not at all the same, and one must be very careful to distinguish between them. Miguel, son of the original settlers, married a Galván, and their son George Antonio, had a daughter who married Ponciano Muñoz. They had nine children who were identified in San Antonio into the early 19th century. Catarina de los Santos, daughter of the original settlers, married Francisco Delgado. Her sister, Josefa, married Juan Galván, son of the well known Commander and his wife, Francisca Xaviera Maldonado.

UANA FRANCISCA PADRON was the daughter of Juan Joseph Padrón and a granddaughter of the original Joseph. Her mother was the daughter of Martín Lorenzo de Armas and María Robaina de Bethencourt. Juana Padrón married the already mentioned, Francisco Xavier Chávez.

T HE CASANOVA family were well known in Spain during the 13th century, when Don Jaime I of Aragón conquered Valencia.

The oldest son of José Pérez (Casanova) and his wife Paula Granado, was Domingo, first *Cabo* in the Presidio of San Antonio in 1779. He married María Concepción de Carvajal, and their son Ignacio was the third of thirteen children.

The sixth child of José Pérez and Paula Granado was ·Juan Ignacio (b. 1756 d. 1823), the well known "Colonel Pérez" who married Clemencia Hernández. Their daughter Gertrudis, born in 1790, married 1st, 1806, Governor Antonio Cordero, and 2nd, 1828, José Cassiano.

José Ignacio Pérez, son of Colonel Pérez, b. 1786, married, 1812, María Josefa Cortinas. Their daughter Josefa married (1855) Jacob Linn.

José Cassiano (Guiseppe Cassini, native of San Remo, of the Republic of Genoa) came to America with a British passport dated 1816, which described him as an "inhabitant of Gibraltar." He took for his second wife, Gertrudis Pérez, widow of the Governor, above mentioned. Their son, José Ignacio, married, 1847, Margarita Rodríguez, daughter of Rufino and Dolores Ruiz. Their daughter Gertrudis was the wife of Charles P. Smith, an ordinance officer in the U. S. A.

José Cassiano married 3rd, in 1833, Margarita Valdez, daughter of José and María Juana Gonzales. Their son José Fermín Cassiano married Tomasa Flores Valdez, daughter of Nicolás Flores and Teresa Valdez; their daughter Teresa married Antonio Pérez. Teresa Valdez, wife of Nicolás Flores, was the daughter of Tomás and Josefa Amondarain. Josefa Amondarain was the daughter of Juan Martín and Josefa Granado. Nicolás Flores was the son of Gaspar, and grandson of Vicente, the son of Francisco Flores and Francisca Travieso.

JOSEFA, the only child of Manuel de Niz, married the oldest son of the widow, María Rodríguez Cabrera. The De Niz family is thus represented by the Rodríguez descendants.

THCMAS, the oldest son of nine children of Vicente Alvarez Travieso and María Ana Curbelo, was the father of Vicente, who married twice and had a large family. A son José had children residing in San Antonio after the middle of the 19th century. Vicenta, Thomas, sister, was the great grandmother of Manuel Yturri and Vicenta Edmunds.

SIMON, the oldest of fifteen children of Francisco de Arocha, and his wife Juana Curbelo, was an army officer. He married a daughter of Joaquín de Urrutia. They had eight children. Miguel, the third, was the grandfather of Lino, who married Encarnación de Urrutia, and whose descendants are well known among the old families of San Antonio.

ANTONIO RODRIGUEZ and Josefa de Niz were the parents of Prudencio, who married Polonia Curbelo. Manuel Ignacio, one of the twelve children of the later, married Antonia Courbiere, and their son Ambrocio was the father of Judge José María Rodríguez, author of the *Memoirs*.

J UAN DELGADO, oldest son of the widow, married a Leal. They had six children. Jacinto, the third, was the father of Clemente, whose daughter Josefa, married José Curbelo, Amador, the sixth, had a very large family. A son José was the father of another Amado, the well known trail driver. He also left many descendants. There were twelve children born to the marriage of Francisco Delgado, second son of the widow, and his wife, Catarina de los Santos. The later descendants of the Delgado are connected with the Travieso and Saucedo. There are many intermarriages with the Tarin and Seguin.

The orphan, Ana Cabrera, married Ignacio de Armas.

T HE GRANADO descendants were identified with their distinguished old home on the plaza. A daughter of Juan de

Acuña, named for the Viceroy, married into the Gortari family, and they had many descendants.

T HE IGNACIO DE ARMAS, whose town grant was north of the parish church, between the two plazas, had seven children. One of their daughters married Francisco Casanova (Pérez), son of Joseph and Paula Granado. Martín de Armas married the widow, María Robaina de Bethencourt. They had four children, of whom, Antonia married Joseph Padrón.

SAN JOSE MISSION

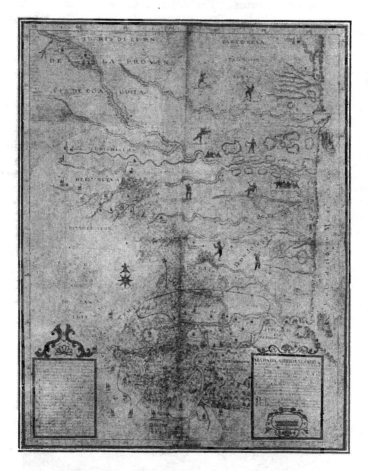

MAPA DE LA SIERRA GORDA Y COSTA DE EL SENO MEXICANO
From Querétaro to La Bahía, by Don Joseph de Escandón, count of Sierra Gorda (1747).

Original, 59 by 75 cm (scale 10 leagues to 4 cm), parchment, in colors; in the Archivo General de Indias, Seville.

APPENDIX

I.

LIST of the MEMBERS

of the

RAMON EXPEDITION OF 1716

WHO REMAINED IN SAN ANTONIO:

Diego Ramón, son of Domingo, m. st, Gertrudis Flores m. 2nd, Teresa Ximénez. Manuel Ramón, nephew of Domingo, from the Presidio of La Bahía, m. Rosalía Martínez; and from them were descended Teresa, wife of Antonio Menchaca, and José, who m. Mariana Leal (her first husband).

Diego (Santiago) Ximénez, Governor of San Antonio de Valero mission in 1720.

María (Suárez) de Longoria, m. Antonio Ximénez.
Juan Zertuche, called "the Alferez of Texas" who m. Josefa Sánchez Navarro; they were godparents in 1720.

Lt. Juan Valdez and his wife María Zapopa, godparents in 1719.
Diego Ximénez Valdez and wife, Antonia Vidales, m. before 1719.

Joseph Galindo and wife, Ana María Ximénez Valdez, had a daughter b. 1720.

Antonio Flores m. María Antonio (de San Miguel) Ximénez; they had a son b. 1720.

Domingo Flores (de Abrego), *Mayordomo* of San Antonio de Valero mission, and wife, Manuela Treviño, had a son b. 1719.

Marcial Saucedo and wife, godparents, 1720.

Lázaro Chirino (Quirino) and wife, Teresa Sánchez Navarro, had a son b. 1720.

Joseph Cadena.
Juan Castro and wife, had a son b. 1720.
Lucas Castro and wife, had a daughter b. 1721.
Joseph Maldonado and family.
Domingo Gonzáles.
Joseph de la Fuente.
Joseph de Montemayor.

Cayetano Pérez, from the Adaes, m. Feliciana de Carvajal before 1724.

APPENDIX

II.

Company, etc.

Dated June 14, 1718

The Staff

(*Plano Mayor*)

The Governor Don Martín de Alarcón

Military Engineer Don Francisco Barreiro y Alvarez
Captain, Alferez, Sergeant and Soldiers:

Santiago Ximenez, Francisco Hernández, Juliano Barrera, Christobal de Carvajal, Vicente Guerra, Sebastián González, Joseph Neyra, Joseph Velásquez, Joseph Ximénez, Antonio Guerra, Gerónimo Carvajal, Ju. Domingo, Joseph Chirino, Ju. Valdez, Francisco R. Francisco Menchaca, Joseph Antonio R., Marcelino Licona, Nicolás Hernández, Francisco Hernández, Andrés de Sosa, Ju. de Castro, Domingo Flores, Joseph Maldonado, Manuel Maldonado, Ju. Galván, Patricio Plácido Flores, Antonio Pérez, Agustín Pérez, Joseph Cadena, Christobal de la Garza, Miguel Hernández, Ju. de Sosa.

All of these were different *Jacte* and the most of them boys, who had not reached the age of fifteen years, and six of them were married and had their *Coyota* and *Mestisa* wives here."

Note: The Carvajal and Hernández families were among the permanent settlers of 1715.

EAST SIDE OF MILITARY PLAZA

APPENDIX

III.

SAN ANTONIO IN 1729

Rosa Guerra was newly wed to Matías Treviño. One of the 17th century cavaliers of Texas was Diego Ximénez Valdez, of Saltillo who had married Antonia Vidales in San Antonio ten years before. Nicolás Flores de Valdez, who had been Alferez in Monclova in 1693, probably a member of the Olivares-Espinosa-Aguirre Expedition, 1709, and who was Captain at San Antonio, being relieved of the command in 1725, was father of Gertrudis, who married Diego Ramón. Martín Flores y Valdez was also one of the principle conquerors and pacifiers of the province of Texas. Marcial Saucedo and his wife, María Ramírez, were early settlers; as were the Gonzáles and Montemayor; and the family of Juan Joseph Rodríguez. Mateo Pérez, who had been in service at the San Francisco Solano Mission as early as 1706, had been Lieutenant at San Antonio previous to 1729. Miguel de la Garza had married María Cantú (1725) and their son was Joseph Joaquín. As early as 1721 Joseph Martínez had married Juana Carvajal. Another newly wed couple were Marcelino Martínez and Alfonza de Castro y Valdez (1728). There were the families of Andrés and Juan de Sosa. In 1719 the master smith, Juan Banul, had come to San Antonio. He was from Brussels,, and his wife, "Madam Banul" and their young family were popular at the time. The Seguin, of distinguished French descent, had come to San Antonio from Aguascalientes in 1722. Two veterans of the Aguayo Expedition were duly respected; they were Juan José de Rojas and Juan Cortinas of Monterrey. The Avila, Núñez-Morillo, and Ocón y Trillo were all prominent at this time.

Three important marriages were celebrated during 1729: that of the master tailor, Andrés de Castro with Antonia Flores; that of the master smith, Cayetano Guerrero with Ana Hernández; and that of Joseph Maldonado with Ana María Ximénez.

Diego Cantú was born during this year; as was Joseph de Luna; Julián Treviño and María Rita Maldonado (married in San Antonio in 1723). Other young people of the place, whose families were to be its leading citizens, were Marcos Guerra, Christobal Chirino, Pedro Nolasco Flores and Miguel Quiñones y Flores de Abrego, all born in San Antonio in 1720. Pedro, the oldest son of Domingo Flores de Abrego, the Mayordomo of the Valero Mission was now ten years of age. His christening had been an event for the frontier life; it was attended by all of the soldiers of the presidio.

Other young people of the community were: the four children of Joseph Ximénez and María Flores Valdez; Ignacio, son of Francisco Flores who married the widow of Gerónimo Carvajal in 1722, Ignacio's mother; and the family of Juan de Castro.

Other prominent citizens of the time were Antonio Ximénez and his wife, María Suárez de Longoria; Juan Zertuche, "the álferez of Texas," and his wife, Josefa Sánchez Navarro; Lieutenant Valdez, "the fiscal," and Gaspar Treviño.—See *San Antonio in* 1729, written by the autor, May, 1929, for the *San Antonio Express.*

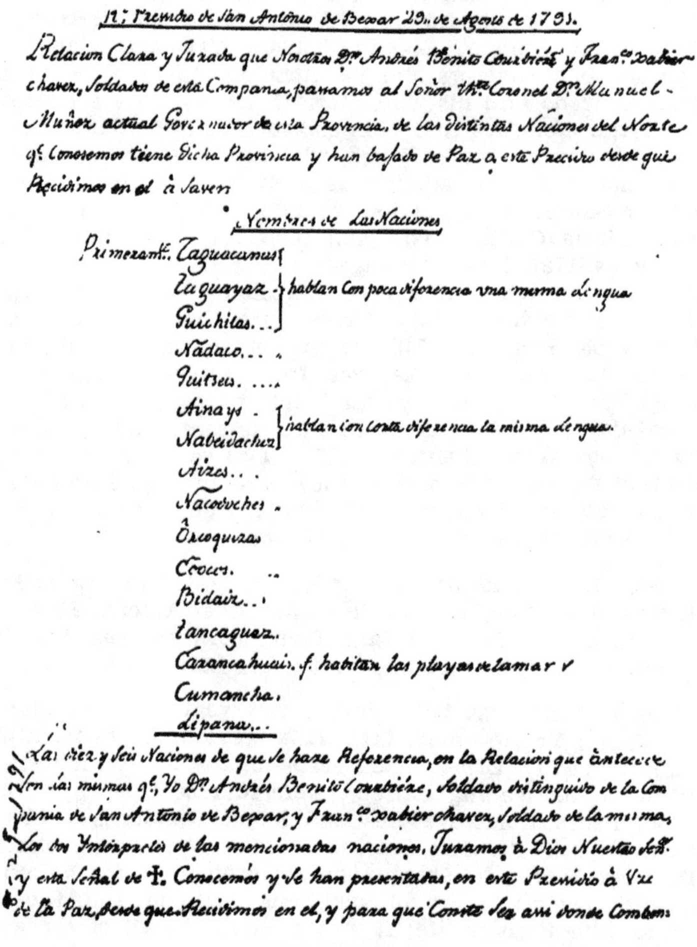
N.° Presidio de San Antonio de Bexar 29. de Agosto de 1791.

Relacion Clara y Jurada que Nosotros Dn. Andrés Benito Courbiere y Fran.co Xabier Chavez, Soldados de esta Compania, pasamos al Señor Then.te Coronel Dn. Manuel Muñoz actual Governador de esta Provincia, de las distintas Naciones del Norte q.e Conosemos tiene Dicha Provincia y han bajado de Paz a este Presidio desde que Recidimos en el á Saver

Nombres de las Naciones

Primeram.te Taguacanas
Tuguayaz } hablan con poca diferencia una misma lengua
Guichitas
Nadaco
Quitseis
Ainays } hablan con corta diferencia la misma lengua
Nabeidachuz
Aizes
Nacodoches
Orcoquizas
Cocos
Bidaiz
Tancaguaz
Carancahuais. habitan las playas de la mar
Cumancha
Lipana

Las diez y Seis Naciones de que se haze Referencia, en la Relacion que antecede Son las mismas q.e Yo Dn. Andrés Benito Courbiere, Soldado distinguido de la Compania de San Antonio de Bexar, y Fran.co Xabier Chavez, Soldado de la misma, Los dos Interpretes de las mencionadas naciones, Juramos á Dios Nuestro Señ.r y esta Señal de ✝. Conocemos y se han presentadas, en este Presidio á Vez de la Paz, desde que Recidimos en el, y para que Conste Sea assi donde Conven

RELACION

Facsimilie of document in Bexar Archives. Andrés Benito Courbiere and Francisco Xavier Chávez, distinguished soldiers of the Presidio of San Antonio de Béxar, to Lt. Col. Don Manuel Muñoz, actual Governor of the Province (August 29, 1791), ennumerating the sixteen Nations of the North who had come to the Presidio in times of peace, during the period of their residence there (Courbiere was from Louisiana, and Chávez from New Mexico).

Index

— D —

— E —

— F —

— G —

— H —

— I —

— J —

Junco y Espriella, 23.
Junta, 9.
Justice, Administration of, 24-25.

— K —

Kadohadacho, 33.
Kampmann, 80.
Karankawa, 32, 38, 39, 49, 69; see Caran-
caguasas.
Kansas, 35.
Kemper, 10.
Kichai, 33.

— L —

Labor of the Adaeseños, 46.
La Bahía, see Bahía.
La Cession, 34.
La Harpe, 49.
Landmarks, 27-28, 75, 80.
Land Office, 11; records, 58.
La Plata, 72.
Larios, Francisco, 23.
La Salle, 17, 32.
Laws, 9, 10, 27.
Leal, 79; family, 81, 83, 85; Joseph, family,
84; Juan Goraz, 84; Juan, el mozo,
family, 83.
Ledger, newspaper, 12.
Leo X., 15.
León, Alonzo de, 7, 16, 17, 66; Juan Ponce
de, 16; Recio, Curate, 75.
Lewis Mill, 56.
Linn, acob, 30, 86; Pérez, 31.
Lipan, 34; 38.
Little Theatre, 78.
Llaneros, 34.
Loguanes, 32.
Longoria, 89.
López, Alberto, 28; de Lois, 19.
Lorenzo de Armas, family, 84.
Loreto, Our Lady of, 20.
Los Ais, 46.
Louis XIV., 15.
Louis, Le Jeune, 16,
Louisiana, 18; Purchase, 27; 32, 33, 92.
Lugo, Col. Carlos de Franquis Benitez,
Governor, 21.
Lungwhitz, H., 56.

Maderos, Antonio Rodríguez, 75, 77.
Mail, 9.
Main Avenue, 80; Plaza, 8, 11, 24, 28-29,
79, 80, 81.
Malaguitos, 32.
Maldonado, 19, 89; Francisca Xaviera, 85.
Manos de Perro, 32.
Manual, text book, 13; by García, 68.
Manzanet, Father, 44, 66.
Map, of 1519, 16; Sierra Gorda, 88.
Maraquites, 67.
Margil, Father, 8, 12, 40, 50, 54.
Market Street, 11, 24, 78, 79.
Marriage Record, first in Archives, 29.
Martinez, 91.
Martos y Navarrete, Gov., 23.
Mata, De La, 9.
Matagorda Bay, 32, 49.
Maverick Home, 11; hotel, 12, Samuel A.,
11; William, 12; 80.
Maximilian, 15.
Mayeye, 34.
Maynes, Francisco, the priest, 29.
Mayors, 11.
Media Villa, 21.
Medina, battle on, 10; 34, 37, 57, 67, 68.
Melián, family, 84.
Menchaca, 19, family, 29; owners of Gov-
ernors' Palace, 30; Diego, 27; Fran-
cisco, 28; José, 29-30; José Antonio,
29; Luis Antonio, 28; Ramón, 89.
Mescaleros, 34.

Mescales, 36.
Metropoli, of New Spain, 54.
Mexico, 7, 8, 9, 11, 13, 15, 16, 17, 34, 47,
54, 68, 72, 73, 74, 83; City, 39.
Milam, Ben., 11.
Military Plaza, 8, 23, 26, 27, 75, 78.
Mill Bridge, 12; Lewis, 12.
Mimbreños, 34.
Mimenim, 35.
Mines, 9.
Minón, Pedro, 28.
Missionaries, 17, 75.
Missions, 8, 12-13, 17, 21, 36, 36-37, 40,
43, 46, 49, 57, 59, 66, 68, 69, 73.
Mississippi River, 16.
Missouri River, 34.
Mitotes, 52.
Moctezuma, 15.
Mogollones, 34.
Monclova, 51.
Montemayor, 89.
Monterrey, 91.
Montes, 30; Rosalia, 27; de Oca, José, 28.
Montevideo, 72.
Morales, Alberto, 27; Don Justo Boneo y,
23.
Morfi, see S.A. missions.
Muñóz, Gov., 25, 26, 46, 69, 92; Father
Peter, 44.
Muruabes, 45.
Muruames, 55.
Music, at San José, 52.
Músquiz, Francisco Decal y, 75; Ramón,
79.

— Mc —

McGloin, 10.
McMullen, 10.

— N —

Nabedache, 66.
Nacachau, 66.
Nacogdoches, 11, 26, 33, 57, 64; archives,
65.
Nacono, 66.
Nadaco, 33, 64.
Naizan, 34.
Narváez, Pánfilo de, 16.
Nasoni, 33.
Nassonites, 33.
Natages, 35.
Natchez Indians, 21.
Natchez, 72.
Natchitoches, 10, 33, 40, 49.
Nations of the North, 9, 92.
Natsoos, 33.
Nava, Pedro de, 25, 69.
Navarrete, Don Angel de Martos y, Gov.,
23.
Navarro, Angel, 28; Juan, 28; home, 28;
Street, 12.
Navisi, 45.
Nazones, 13, 64.
Nebedache, 33.
Neche, 66; mounds, 66.
Neches Indians, 13; San Francisco de los,
66.
Neches River, 66.
Netchez, 32.
New Mexico, 21, 35, 92.
New Philippines, 26, 50.
Newspapers, 12.
Niz, De, 80; family, 83; 84, 86; Rodríguez,
86.
Nolan, Philip, in S.A., 26; prisoners, 26.
Nueces River, 32, 34, 36, 66.
Nuestro Padre San Francisco de los Téjas,
66; Espada, 68.
Nueva Estremadura, 50.
Nuevo León, 17; 22, 23.
Núñez, 29; Morillo, family, 28, 91.

— T —

CPSIA information can be obtained
at www.ICGtesting.com
Printed in the USA
BVHW090044030223
657724BV00007B/419